EROTIC TESTIMONIES

SUNY series in Black Women's Wellness

Stephanie Y. Evans, editor

EROTIC TESTIMONIES

BLACK WOMEN DARING TO BE WILD AND FREE

JULIA S. JORDAN-ZACHERY

Cover, *Three women seated outside of a door dressed in blue* by Erin X. Smithers. Used with permission.

Published by State University of New York Press, Albany

Printed in the United States of America

For information, contact State University of New York Press, Albany, NY
www.sunypress.edu

Library of Congress Cataloging-in-Publication Data

Name: Jordan-Zachery, Julia S., 1971– author.
Title: Erotic testimonies : Black women daring to be wild and free / Julia S. Jordan-Zachery.
Description: Albany : State University of New York Press, [2022] | Series: SUNY series in Black women's wellness | Includes bibliographical references and index.
Identifiers: LCCN 2022014100 | ISBN 9781438491172 (hardcover : alk. paper) | ISBN 9781438491189 (ebook)
Subjects: LCSH: Womanism. | Feminist criticism. | African American women. | Women, Black.
Classification: LCC HQ1197 .J67 2022 | DDC 305.4201—dc23/eng/20220404
LC record available at https://lccn.loc.gov/2022014100

10 9 8 7 6 5 4 3 2 1

These words are dedicated to Kathleen Griffith.

Contents

Acknowledgments

One never writes a book alone, and this one is no exception. The book is genuinely birthed from a Black feminist praxis of community. And that community is vast; I apologize if I miss anyone. My dear friend Russell helped me to vision this book. He listened to me talk about it from its early conceptualization, always encouraging me to write. In the early stages of the pandemic, I joined a Black women's writing group; we initially committed to writing for six weeks which eventually made its way into twelve weeks—thanks to the organizers and all who showed up to hold space. Some of us continued past this, meeting Monday through Friday to write. Through laughter and some much sista-girl encouragement, Angela Lewis, Deidre Flowers, Leta Hopper, Danielle Cooper, and Courtney Buggs stood beside me as I wrote. Michelle Meggs would listen to me talk about this book on our walks. And every night, Monday to Friday, I would text Janine Holc—accountability truly works, much gratitude. And then there is Celeste Henery, who ever so gently pushed me to focus on the book's central point. Thanks, Celeste, for your gentleness and grace. Wendy Grossman, thanks to the protest in little old RI. To the reviewers, much gratitude for your thoughtfulness. To my mother, Monica Jordan, and my grandmother, Kathleen Griffith, thank you for always being in my corner. Thanks, dad, Evan Jordan, for allowing me to dream. Then there is my ray of sunshine Makeen Zachery whose quiet strength supported me throughout this journey. Thanks, gurl ☺. Finally, thanks to the ancestors for holding my words and graciously offering them back to me.

Acknowledgments

Feeling, and Deeply

A Source of Knowledge

The uses of the erotic, according to Audre Lorde (1978), can be liberatory. I repeatedly read her essay "Uses of the Erotic: The Erotic as Power" trying to determine how I could use my erotic. Particularly, I wondered how to use my erotic as a means of living with and through race-gender violence. Lorde's writing was part of the sacred texts I relied on during what, for me, was a very challenging time given the race-gender targeting I faced. During this time, I wanted to learn how to be—how to exist in this world as a Black woman. And so, I sought to see Black women, and I selected works by Black women that allowed me to see how they managed being Black and woman. Lorde's essay invited me to go into my interior, to dwell with the feelings that resided there, and to use the knowledge to live my truth. Over time, truth living became my interpretation of "Uses of the Erotic." And, as I show in *Erotic Testimonies: Black Women Daring to Be Wild and Free*, we access this truth living by going into the interior, experiencing our feelings, and taking the knowledge these feelings offer to come into the world—a world that sometimes tries to violently expel Black women. And it is through truth living that Black women can be wild and access the liberation that Lorde discusses in "Uses of the Erotic."

In *Erotic Testimonies*, Lorde's "Uses of the Erotic" serves as a springboard for seeing Black women and the work they do to venture into their interior—what Lorde refers to as the deeply feminine spiritual plane. In essence, I riff off "Uses of the Erotic" to explore how Black women use feelings, accessed by going into the interior, to engage in the process of self-actualization. As such, this is a book on Black women's interiority and the knowledge that rests there, and how they use this knowledge to see themselves to make themselves real. At its core, I offer you a book about feeling and feeling deeply and trusting that these feelings have knowledge that helps Black women move toward self-actualization and ultimately freedom.

~

The story that I present to you, via Black women's testimonies, does not want to be defined. Yet here I am trying. A part of me is resisting having to define this book. I sense that my resistance results from the feeling that I need to draw lines to neatly place this book on wild Black women into. And I wonder: Am I resisting simply for the sake of resisting? The spirit tells me no to this query.[1] Thus, I come back to this notion of lines and how I am stuck when I sit to write, particularly on defining/finding a scholarly home for this project. *Erotic Testimonies: Black Women Daring to Be Wild and Free* is neither about theory nor practice. I settle on an interpretive journey when forced to find words, but this is not a "standard" academic genre. In part, it is because this book is not genre-specific. It is a generative project—a way of seeing Black women.

This generative project is an interpretive journey into Black women's interiority by engaging in a performative embodied reading of the testimonies offered by four wild women. Through this practice of performative embodied reading, I am able to develop meaning as I operate from a place of intimate relating—a model of testifying that I learned from my grandmother. *Erotic Testimonies* is the testimony of the individual, but more importantly, it is a testimony of how the individual speaks to the collective. It offers us an opportunity to see Black women and how they give birth to themselves and each other. And this is where my gran becomes relevant. Hers is one of the early testimonies of Black women's self-actualization I bore witness to. My grandmother, now ninety-three, like other women in my life, first introduced me to the praxis and embodiment of Black womanhood/feminism without ever uttering the words praxis, Black feminism, methodology, or epistemology. Thus, she influences how I approach this performative embodied reading in my attempt to see Black women. The performance of seeing Black women spreading across these pages is not linear, just like my gran's testimonies. While my gran's testimonies allowed me to see her, a glimpse into her interior, they also were provocative in the sense that they asked me to see me. Over time, I have come to appreciate that my gran's testimonies were always filled with feelings, deep feelings. She showed me how feelings are filled with knowledge, even before I turned to Audre Lorde's writings.

In speaking of the knowledge of feelings, Audre Lorde writes, "All I had was the sense that I had to hold on to these feelings and that I had to air them in some way" (1984, 88). As suggested by Lorde, feelings provide access to a knowledge that is "that dark and true depth which understanding serves, waits upon, and makes accessible through language to ourselves and others" (1984, 68). For Lorde, feelings can be expressed through poetry, for example, but interestingly, they need not depend on understanding. In a conversation with Adrienne Rich, who asked Lorde to help her understand, Lorde (1984, 105) responded, "I don't know about you, Adrienne, but I have a difficult enough time making my perceptions verbal, tapping that deep place, forming that handle, and documentation at that point is often useless. Perceptions precede analysis just as visions precede action or accomplishments." Feelings can stand separate from understanding. And feelings are filled with knowledge.

Our interiority is the portal to our feelings, and as such, it is filled with knowledge. This project is not about discovering or enabling the marginalized to speak. These women, like all Black women, have a voice. I am less concerned about if they offer an authentic voice. Instead, I find myself curious about their self-actualization. This requires finding and using epistemic resources that rest on the interior. Thus, the "approach" of performative embodied reading. Performative embodied reading is situated in the lineage of Black feminist thought, where it is argued that Black women seek to make themselves visible via their lived experiences (see Collins 2000; hooks 1989a) by accessing their feelings (see Baker-Bell 2017; Brown 2013) as they seek freedom (see Stewart and Breeden 2021; Cooper 2018).

A performative embodied reading recognizes that the body is a site of knowledge; it is flexible, reflective, responsive, participatory, and political. As Dwight Conquergood (1991, 180) states, embodiment is "an intensely sensuous way of knowing." I go into my interior to access this sensuous way of knowing. Engaging in a performative embodied reading relies on the notion that our bodies are not neutral. Our bodies offer a way of being while resisting other ways that may be grounded in negative race-gender stereotypes.

The body serves as an exploratory tool allowing me to engage with and be in relationship with the testimonies offered. I listen, like the women who offer their testimonies, to what my body and theirs come to know.

Using that knowledge, I probe the testimonies offered to make meaning of how Black women engage in the process of self-actualization in their quest for freedom. This approach allowed me to see how these women use feelings to engage in self-actualization and how they understand what it means to be a wild Black woman. And what I learned is that these women's self-actualization offers them a sense of freedom. Freedom is in the feelings and in the capacity to feel deeply. These feelings help us address disembodiment resulting from living in and with multiple oppressive structures and behaviors. Feelings lie in the interior, the place where the erotic rests—that place of truth. And when we access that truth and choose to live that truth, it can lead us to actions that can free us.

As I engaged in the performative embodied reading of the testimonies, I kept in the back of my mind, "who are you accountable to?" I am accountable to Audre Lorde and all she imagined, experienced, and argued for. When I think of what Audre Lorde did, express her feelings in hopes that they would lead us to action—self-actualization—I think of freedom. Beyond Ms. Lorde, I'm also accountable to my grandmother, Kathleen Griffith, as she saw me before I even saw me. And I am accountable to Black women.

Erotic Testimonies is my ode to Black women!

Chapter 1

Testifying

An Introduction

Prelude I

Tanisha Anderson,
Yvette Smith,
Rekia Boyd,
Natasha McKenna,
Sandra Bland,
Kindra Chapman,
Kimberlee Randle-King,
Joyce Curnell,
Ralkina Jones,
Kayla Moore,
Gynnya McMillen,
Korryn Gaines.
. . .

I name you all and those other Black femmes, girls, and women we have lost as a result of structural/state/quasi-state/individual race-gender violence. I open *Erotic Testimonies: Black Women Daring to Be Wild and Free* with a personal ritual that I use to honor those women who have been stolen from us, from society. I name them. I name these women in hopes that one day we will all be free. Free to live our lives as sovereign beings. My performance of this ritual, of honoring Black women, is part of my testifying. Testifying is one vehicle I use to live my erotic—that is, my truth. This is my testimony.

This is a book about testifying. Specifically, *Erotic Testimonies* is a book on Black women's acts of testifying and their notes of freedom.

~

> Freeing yourself was one thing, claiming ownership of that freed self was another.
>
> —Toni Morrison, *Beloved*, 111–112

What does it mean to be a free Black woman? As we experience COVID-19 and the police brutality pandemics and an economic recession, which are all comingling with preexisting forms of structural violence, what does it mean to be a free Black woman?

Summer 2020, I spend what feels like countless hours sitting on my back porch reading the words of Toni Morrison, Alice Walker, bell hooks, and Audre Lorde, among others. To be specific, I search their words, curiously and fervently looking for how they define and talk about freedom and Black feminine freedom. It seems that we are entering into what for my generation will be our Red Summer—state-sanctioned murders of Black and Brown folk and global resistance to such (for more on the Red Summer of 1919, see Ewing 2019). It is our summer, a summer filled with pandemics that have us sheltering in place as we seek to understand how to protect our minds, bodies, and spirits from the harm of COVID-19 and the harm resulting from race-gender violence while simultaneously protesting against such violence. My understanding of race-gender violence suggests that it is structural, physical, and emotional violence intended to cause harm, hurt, or kill an individual's physical body and soul, based on the simultaneity of their embodied race and gender. So, how do I, as a Black woman, find freedom in the midst of not just this moment, but what for me, like other Black individuals, is a long history of resisting our annihilation? As I sat on my back porch in summer 2020, I was reminded of all those days and nights when I sat in the dark wondering how I was to survive the habitual race-gender violence I faced for ten long years.

I sit and read.
Words blur as tears trickle down my cheeks
splashing against the page.
Words, like my thoughts
become murky, so
I let my mind wander,
imagining a space of freedom and ease.
A place that does not require me to fight for survival.
I enter my interior, and I find rest.

That is what it feels like at times, like I am in a constant state of fighting for the existence of a sovereign Black personhood. To help ease the pain of it all, I created altars where I remember the Black women, known and unknown, who fought for my freedom. I remind myself of the value of my personhood by reading the sacred texts of Black women, written by those I name above among others. They offer me their testimony; whether it is in the form of fiction, poetry, biomythography, song, choreopoem, prose, or some other form, Black women have recorded their testimonies and how they seek freedom. The testimonies they offer me (and us) lie in the erotic, which is that place that is deep in the interior of the Black feminine divine—that place of truth. Through their testimonies, I enter into my interior.

In 1978 Audre Lorde authored the celebrated and often cited essay "Uses of the Erotic: The Erotic as Power"—it was first presented as a talk at the Fourth Berkshire Conference on History of Women, Mount Holyoke College. Since then, many have cited this essay, and it has informed much research (McLauchlan 2018; Young 2012; Molina, 1994). However, to date, no full-length work explores how Black-identified women engage their erotic. Lorde (1984, 57) forcefully writes, "Our erotic knowledge empowers us, becomes a lens through which we scrutinize all aspects of our existence, forcing us to evaluate those aspects honestly in terms of their relative meaning within our lives." Engaging the erotic, for Lorde, was a way to ignite the self to facilitate social transformations. The self that Lorde references is not "the self of liberal individualism" and neither is it used to maintain or prop up neoliberal social formations or ideologies (Bambara 1983, 13). Instead, the self is an "aesthetics of existence" which is used for the abolition of oppressive structures and for the liberation of those who face systemic oppression (Bambara 1983, 13). Consequently, the erotic is simultaneously a technique of the self and a social practice available when Black women tap into their interior—that place of truth.[1]

> *A place of*[2]
> "our deepest and nonrational knowledge"
> *that personifies* "creative power and harmony."
> A "well of replenishing and provocative force."
> *It is the* "life force of women."
> *Available to the woman*
> "who does not fear its revelation."
> *It is that*
> "internal sense of satisfaction" *that once*
> *experienced,*
> *Our work*
> "becomes a conscious decision."
> *So, we can no longer*
> *separate the spiritual from the political nor the sensual.*
> *The erotic,* "our deepest knowledge."
> "empowers us."
> *Functioning,*
> *by* "forcing us to evaluate those aspects *of our lives* honestly."
> "Flow[ing] and color[ing] *our* lives with a kind of energy"
> that "heightens and sensitizes and strengthens all [our] experiences."
> *So that our actions* "against oppression."
> *take on a new tenor.* So that we
> "become
> integral with self,
> motivated and,
> empowered from within."[3]

Not only does Audre Lorde inform us about how the erotic functions, but she tells us how the erotic functions in her life. Her testimony informs us that the erotic functions

1. by "providing the power which comes from sharing deeply any pursuit with another person,"

and

2. by “the open and fearless underlining of my capacity for joy” (Lorde 1984, 56)

In “Uses of the Erotic: The Erotic as Power,” Audre Lorde offers an aesthetic of being at an individual and collective level. *Erotic Testimonies: Black Women Daring to be Wild and Free*, like a jazz song, riffs Lorde’s concept of the erotic to explore Black women’s use of it in the face of race-gender violence. And through their testimonies, I delve into how they dare to live wild and free.

How and why am I connecting the uses of the erotic, the interior, truth-telling, and testimony? And what does any of this have to do with “wild” and free Black women? Lorde (1984) tells us,

> When we live outside ourselves, and by that I mean on external directives only rather than from our internal knowledge and needs, when we live away from those erotic guides from within ourselves, then our lives are limited by external and alien forms, and we conform to the needs of a structure that is not based on human need, let alone an individual’s. (58)

Audre Lorde offers a way of being/existing in the world that calls on us to know our truths deeply. We come to know that truth by going into the interior of our being and using that, the erotic—our deepest feelings—as a way of organizing our lives. Through the use of our erotic, we can engage in self-articulation and self-actualization. This self-articulation and self-actualization are then shared in community, via testimony, through our words and our deeds. And this is how we begin to effect change at both an individual and communal level.

~

In this book, I seek to tell the story of how four Black women live their erotic—recognizing that the *I* they reference is also part of the collective *we*—and how they use self, individual and collective, to resist and create change. What makes these women “wild”? Using Black feminism’s understanding of interiority, I understand being a wild woman as one who uses an intuitive spiritual approach, that deep “female and spiritual plane,” referenced by Lorde, and its sensuousness to heal from oppressive structures. I understand that “female and spiritual plane” as our interior, the place where our feelings reside. When we can access our interior, which requires work and often hard work, then there is an opportunity to align body, mind, and spirit to live an understanding of oneself that (sometimes) allows us to live outside of the often prototypical, stereotypical, or socially sanctioned understanding of Black womanhood, whether that is an understanding of the "respectable" Black woman, the "angry" Black woman, the "welfare queen" Black woman, and the list continues. It is in this space, the interior, that the women who testify here become wild.

Although Audre Lorde does not employ the term *wild woman* in her often-cited piece "Uses of the Erotic: The Erotic as Power," she writes, "the erotic is a resource within each of us that lies in a deeply female and spiritual plane, firmly rooted in the power of our unexpressed or unrecognized feelings" (1984, 53). *Wild woman*, as a concept, is my interpretation of how Lorde suggests that the erotic is grounded in aligning one's inner truth with one's outward endeavors. She says that when women live their erotic (outside the expectations of womanhood), they are often feared,

> The fear of our desires keeps them suspect and indiscriminately powerful, for to suppress any truth is to give it strength beyond endurance. The fear that we cannot grow beyond whatever distortions we may find within ourselves keeps us docile and loyal and obedient, externally defined, and leads us to accept many facets of our oppression as women. (Lorde 1984, 57–58)

Furthermore, Lorde cautions us not to reduce the erotic only to the sexual plane. To that end, she writes, "So we are taught to separate the erotic demand from most vital areas of our lives other than sex" (Lorde 1984, 55). Consequently, when the erotic is only rested on the plane of sex, Lorde implores us to recognize that dissatisfaction sets in.

The women who share their testimonies in this book on Black women's feelings seemingly embody Audre Lorde's understanding of the uses of the erotic.[4] One woman uses yoga and Judaism as part of her understanding of self. A second woman exists in a queer space, has experienced sexual violence, and uses this as her entry into race-gender-sexuality-class organizing. And then there is the Black woman who is a Shaman storyteller. For the fourth individual, I opted to tell the story of a Black femme-identified witch. Working their way through state and culturally sanctioned religions, this individual has found respite being a witch. Before this project, these women were known to me—either directly or indirectly. For the most part, they all have a public presence because of the work that they do—to build community. In fact, of the four women, only one is known to me indirectly—I came across her work and was intrigued by how she articulated her life as a witch. In their way, and as they share their truths, these women have allowed me to come deeper into my erotic. In chapters 3 through 6, I introduce these women in more detail. But why should you even care about the testimonies of these women? The testimonies "become pedagogical and transformative [thereby] opening a space for personal healing, public dialogue, and policy changes" (Spry 2011, 56). Beyond this, these four Black women's testimonies help us advance Black feminist thought.

~

Erotic Testimonies is written in a manner that resonates from my erotic. In 2019 I wrote,

> I also exit in terms of the nature of the research I engage in and how I choose to write—as represented, for example, in this piece. I write this piece without some of the usual elements that tend to accompany academic writings. For example, I use, minimally, headings and subheadings. As I have grown as an academic, I have grappled with why this form of writing has never sat well with me. It always felt that performing my writing in a particular manner reinscribed Western notions of knowledge production and the ways of translating "knowledge." Beyond this, I simply wanted to write this part of my story on my relationship with academia in a way that was reflective of my identity—a Black woman from Barbados—and how the women like my grand-mother often told their stories and how they developed theory based on lived realities to challenge power structures. (72)

Consequently, this project is written to mirror the testimonies told by my grandmother. The way she and other Black women would testify could result in a tale stretched over time and space—elements offered at different times, constructing a whole while often leaving holes. The testimonies would meander, like a river, trickling or gushing at different times as my gran opted to reveal what she chose to reveal. Her testimonies were sometimes peppered with different Bajan sayings—some familiar and some less so, often leaving me to wonder did she make that up in the moment. I would sometimes laugh or become somber based on the nature of the testimony and how she chose to tell it. But I was always delighted when my gran decided to offer a testimony that allowed me a glimpse into her interior. In the manner in which my gran would share her testimonies, this work is written in such a way as to be more evocative as opposed to descriptive (Prendergast, Leggo, and Sameshima 2009; Leggo 2008). I sincerely hope that you engage the project through a lens of "think with," as opposed to "think about," the testimonies of the women offered here (Ellis and Bochner 2000, 735). In other words, I invite you to become a part of the testimony, to engage in your own performative embodied reading. As you read, think alongside us about how you enter your erotic. This allows for *Erotic Testimonies* to become a shared creation where we can see each other—individually and collectively.

Erotic Testimonies is a project about creating and analyzing—what I think of as an interpretive journey. It brings together social science, conventional academic writing, and the arts as a means of challenging these demarcations we often encounter in society. This is a genre-blending text. I use poetry, a blend of my words and the words of authors, to talk about theory and the approach to this "study" as a means of situating *Erotic Testimonies* in the lineage of Black feminist thinking and doing. As a reminder, I italicize my words to set them apart from direct quotes which are indicated with quotation marks, and citations are offered in footnotes so as not to disrupt the poetry. I do this as

> *Black feminist writers tell us to*
> dismantle the master's house[5]
> *But not with his tools*
> *If we want to be able to*
> *Move*
> From the margin to the center.[6]
> So, we write in our invented genres
> exploit[ing] "unconventional citation styles."[7]
> *Cause, this is how we get*
> *free.*

Consequently, I offer you this interpretive journey. As Elaine Richardson (2003, 82) says, "The Black woman's consciousness of her condition/ing, her position/ing in American society, the condition/ing of her audiences must be factored into her language and literacy practices." When I factor in my/our language, this project in its own way becomes wild, mirroring the inventiveness of the women who inform it.

Sometimes We Moan: A Way of Entering the Interior

Testimony,
holding our feminine energy,
is both personal and political.
It is sensuous and liberating.

As a little girl sitting in the Church of God in Welchman Hall, St. Thomas, Barbados, I would often witness those answering the call to give a testimony. Mainly, women would stand and testify of how good God had been to them or a family member. Testimonies of "God saved me . . ." and "I'm here by the grace of God to tell you of God's mercy . . ." peppered the air. These testimonies were often mingled with eruptions of "Praise God" and the deep, deep moans of those who bore witness to the testimony.

Outside of church, I got to witness my gran give her testimony. In the middle of completing a task, she would sometimes declare, "Thank you, Jesus!" It sometimes felt random; I was a little girl witnessing her testifying. But what I learned from my gran was that those outbursts were part of her internal dialogue. They reflected that internal place where only she had the privilege of seeing, feeling, and experiencing. But ever so often, the internal would come to the surface and burst forth like a flower budding early in the dawn. It was always there, just the form of it all changed. So, I learned from my gran that we, at least some of us, are always testifying (and that testifying is not simply religious). My grandmother taught me a lot about testifying, and long before I ever explored it as an approach that I would one day rely on as part of my work on telling Black women's stories. And so, I find myself depending on what my gran taught me as an epistemology/practice of how Black women testify. I rely on this knowledge and that knowledge written by and about Black women to speak on the epistemology of testimony. As a practice of collecting and sharing the testimony of the women who graciously shared theirs, I understand that:

1. Testifying allows that which is on the interior to be shared—with others, God, or just the universe;
2. The testifier has control over what is shared and how. They are the narrators of their story, and as such, their testimony need not be interpreted or changed; and
3. As the recipient of the testimony, I have agency in how I can engage. I can declare "amen," moan, or simply remain silent, taking only what I need and offering only what is available to me—as such, testifying is a dialectical practice.

The testimony of the Black women who inform *Erotic Testimonies* is a blend of the emotional, mystical, and physical. As Lorde describes in "Uses of the Erotic," the erotic is multidimensional including the political, sensuousness, and spirituality. The testimonies I listened to and interacted with are that same blend that I witnessed sitting in the pews of the Church of God and the same blend that layered my gran's utterances. These utterances were a part of my gran's process of self-actualization.

Black feminist thought often explores the notion of social images and how they are read vis-à-vis Black womanhood. They also analyze/study how Black women work to "create," self-actualize, themselves in light of race-gender-class-sexuality-religion and other oppressive structures and often negative social images. While it is often implied that this creation of self is an internal project—that place in the interior that this study explores—one can also examine that creation as an external project. Self-creation can become an external project when women live the erotic in their day to day, their activism, and their way of being in the world—what literature refers to as praxis (see Taylor 1998). Thus, bringing together these elements of self-actualization—the internal and external—is a way of exploring how these women understand the erotic and how they dare to live the erotic.

I attempt to tap into the interior, the place where the erotic resides, by asking each woman to reflect on the following words: wild, interior, divine, feminine, energy, and erotic (words extracted, in part, from Lorde's writings). These words serve as cues, highlighting emotional standpoints of moments of transformation and decision-making that are located in the feeling body as opposed to the external world. One can imagine these words as creating a container of sorts to go within. This process was not an interview as traditionally understood but more of a think-with process. Wild, interior, divine, feminine, energy, and erotic were selected as they allowed us to give language to feeling states—what can be a really vulnerable space. As I posed the words, the four Black women, in the moment, engaged in a process of think and feel. Consequently, the responses were spontaneous and, at times, raw. I was able to see the movement of their thoughts and the feelings they elicited as they flowed with and through the words. Being in this space with these women required a type of trust and respect—all nurtured and nourished given our shared interest in truth, justice, and liberation.

The testimonies they share may meander in a way that makes sense to them. My role as the holder of the testimony is less to analyze it for themes and more so to offer the reader a rendition of the truths, alongside my truth, that are shared with me. Janette Taylor (1998, 59) writes, "It is not enough to just collect narrative data; rather, we must attempt to locate ourselves and perform research in ways that affirm African American women." To this end, Taylor suggests the use of testimony as a means for not only locating oneself but also affirming African American women. This is how we get to the context-specific knowledge (grounded in feelings) held by Black women (also thought of as their standpoint) because "as informants, Black women are no longer simply talked to, but talk for themselves" (Few, Stephens, and Rouse-Arnett 2003, 207). A tradition of Black feminism is that Black women should be allowed to speak not just about their experiences but also speak from their own experiences (Collins 2000).

Consequently, I did not massage and/or shape their stories in any way but instead received the testimony and shared it with the reader. And this is where Gloria Anzaldúa becomes valuable as I organize how to present the testimonies of the four women. As Anzaldúa (1990 cautions,

> Let the reader beware—I here and now issue a caveat perusor: s/he must do the work of piecing this text together. . . . As the perspective and focus shift, as the topics shift, the listener/reader is forced into participating in the making of meaning—she is forced to connect the dots, to connect the fragments. (xviii)

This approach may challenge academic norms. The same norms that were not necessarily designed to accommodate Black women and our ways of knowing, but that we are expected to follow when we write our stories.

"Gaining insight into the everyday lives of African-American women and how they interpret them requires conscious methodological approaches and research practices." (Mullings 2000, 20) When this project first came to me, I knew that I could not simply use the methods I had been trained in as an economist or political scientist. Such training seems to go against what this book on testimonies was calling for. I needed a "conscious methodological approach and research practice," and so I searched beyond my "disciplines" learning how to un-discipline myself in the process. Eventually, I found a model of how to do this work—of how to engage with testimony in a way that allowed my voice to fade into the background or to simply play a supporting role—like the women who would call out "amen" as another testified. So, I borrowed from others to compose how I respond to the testimonies shared (my process of intimate relation) and how I present the testimonies. From Marya Sosulski, Nicole Buchanan, and Chandra Donnell (2010), I got the following:

1. "Privilege the voices of the narrators and their "interpretations by examining their actual language and symbolic meaning and presents an overview of the connections the narrators make as they weave their stories into the whole narrative construction." (37)

Janette Taylor (2005) contributed,

> Except a few sentences, only minor editing has been done when necessary to clarify the women's words. The results may be read as a sequence of

2. "intersecting or interwoven stories contained under a theme that represents the collective voice or as single or separate ideas." (1479)

I pay attention to what the women return to in telling their stories. I also pay attention to the utterances that may not be picked up and repeated but are offered, as they too are important to the testimony. Finally, as this is an embodied performative reading, I pay attention to my responses, how I think with the testimonies. Combined, they offer a multilayered, textually rich testimony.

I was trying to fit these "wild Black women" into a particular format for this book. And I could not see it. I simply could not get it done. It was because they were screaming *no* the whole time as I tried to stuff the women into something they did not want to be. "I'm listening, ya'll."

I put the project down and went for a walk. During this walk, I had a meeting with Audre Lorde. It went something like this:

> ME: Audre, I don't know what to do. I genuinely don't know what to do with these testimonies. Any thoughts?
>
> AUDRE: [silence]
>
> ME: Well, I guess I'll let it be.
>
> AUDRE: Talk to your ancestors. Invite in the spirits.
>
> ME: I thought that's what I was doing.
>
> AUDRE: I write about Black goddesses and spirits. Let them guide you.

I continued my walk, trusting that this would make sense. But I could not help but wonder how one can use the ancestors and spirits to guide "analysis"? This did not fit anything I had been trained to do.

Eventually, it did. Audre Lorde was invoking the sacred and ancient spirituality. Karla Holloway (1992, 2) says, "It is through the ancient spirituality of this (African-American) literature that the unity of soul and gender is not challenged but is recovered and celebrated. Within this spirituality, the recovered metaphor that articulates the relationship between soul and gender is the metaphor of the goddess/ancestor."

Lorde's body of work reflects her engagement with the sacred and mystical, illustrating how she centers Black feminine power and how it works to imagine and create a more just society. Often, Lorde intersects the spiritual/mystical with collective power movement by drawing on West African goddesses. In the poem "A Woman Speaks," Lorde references the "witches of Dahomey," a type of nod to Vodoun, a West African religious practice. She speaks of how Black goddesses, which also reside in Black women, will rise with "magic" that is "unwritten" and indeed unknown.

> Lorde speaks of
> Orishala/Eshu/Mother Yemonja,
> how she and the "beautiful Oshun . . . lie down together"[8]
> Oya

And of
Eshidale's priests, whom she tells us, will be "very busy" in
their work of righting wrongs.[9]

Ancestral Black feminine spirit energies and power are centered, bringing together the spiritual and material worlds. Lorde is recovering their voices in the face of white normativity that privileges one way of knowing, thus articulating the relationship that Holloway speaks of. She inserts the past into our prospects of the future by showing us a different way of knowing in the present. Presented to us by Lorde is a way of knowing that is grounded in Black women's subjectivity. And it is through this knowing that Black women can cultivate a whole self, a whole Black women self, that stands outside of constructed distinctions.

My challenge is that I wanted to have the women fit into chapters organized around the words that I used in our conversations. This approach was not working, and I do not know why. After that conversation with Audre Lorde, I listened to my ancestors and decided to give each woman their own story. In a conversation with a friend, she described it this way (and I'm paraphrasing). There is no need to blend the women into one. Each has her essence, their own story; every rainbow has a blend of colors where each color ends and the other begins. The essence of these women is that they each have their own story and experiences, and they stand in them flat-footed. The blend you are seeking is in their essence. So, while I asked each woman to respond to a series of words, I seek not to blend their responses because to do such is to dilute a bit of her essence.

And I offer no analysis of their words, but instead, I offer my "field notes" and the notes I took in the margins as I read and reread the transcripts. These notes capture what I mean by performative embodied reading. The titles of the chapters are based on the words of the women and what resonated with my spirit during and even after our conversation. And I did what Audre Lorde instructed me to do. I went back to her writings on Black goddesses and spirits and sat for a long time until the "method" came to me. I allowed the spirit and the ancestors to guide the write-up of each chapter. Each woman was presented to me either in a color, sound/song, or texture, along with some quality that I later researched and matched to African mythology. Teal and Yemaya, alongside the song "Window Seat" by Eryka Badu, guides the write-up of Maya. Red, and not some bright red, but this intense red color that seems to have traces of black and other colors mixed in, and the African goddess Ashiakle and crescent moons inform the write-up of Sekile. The spirit of Oshun guided my write-up of Val, and when I hear Val, I hear rain, the steady beat of raindrops hitting the once upon a time tin roofs that covered homes in Barbados. For Lakeesha, the color green and Oya capture her essence.

When the Author Testifies

i long

i long to write, but in different ways.
allowing all parts of me to come
together,
creating that genre that has yet to be named.
I long to write,
in a way that defies Western Ideology,
using words and symbols that are yet known.
i long, to write.

This is the space where I offer up a bit of my testimony—what is often termed autoethnography in the academy. I offer autoethnographic poems as a way of thinking of how I began the process of entering into my interior to discover and live my erotic.

The above poem, "i long," is part of my testimony of living with race-gender violence and my struggle to find myself in the midst of it all. At some point in our lives, Black women experience race-gender violence either directly or indirectly. We are subjected to the murders of Koryn Gaines, Trayvon Martin, Tamir Rice, . . . We are subjected to what those in power now term *microaggressions*, those insidious acts of what I term racism that we experience in our daily lives. Well, I lived with all of that in addition to repeated attacks against my Black womanhood (Jordan-Zachery 2019). As we say in Barbados, my tongue is tied in telling the stories of all of my experiences. But what I can tell you is that my experience was insidious and raised to a level that I had never experienced before. I eventually termed my experiences with the race-gender violence I faced "the swamp." Although my experience was tangible, it was reflected in my mind, body, and spirit; I needed something to help me visualize it all. So, I drew it, and I wrote,

The swamp is
"institutional betrayal."[10]
that place of evil
where soul murder[11] is committed . . .
a form of containment
seeking to limit me.
Soul Murder

I kept thinking of the idea and ideography of "soul murder" as a method for articulating my experience as I was left feeling like a shell of myself. All that I loved was seemingly stripped away from me. My words, my hair, my sense of being grounded. All gone as a result of race-gender violence.

While it was hard for me to manage all that I experienced, it was especially hard to manage not writing.

Watching my words escape
or maybe
laying dormant
inaccessible regardless.
Phantom pain
becoming all too real,
I sit, longing to write.
Yet, the English language fails me.
The language given to me,
or forced upon me
as I didn't have a choice
but to learn the language of my colonizer.
I find myself trapped,
wanting to utter words
but muted.
The words escaping me.
Or maybe,
laying dormant.
Inaccessible regardless.

How can I be an academic and not write? How can I be a lover of words and not write? I have always loved words. As a little girl, I remember how I would lie next to my mother, an avid reader, and "read" alongside her. I was maybe two or three, or somewhere in between those ages. We would lie next to each other, on our backs with our knees bent, reading. When she turned her page, I turned my page. Captivated. Linked together by words on a page, falling in love with words and my mother, I would lie there. Entering into my feeling body. My mother tells the story of how she came to pick me up from "school" one day only to find me in tears. I was around three years old and had begged to go to school. As she tells the story, she rushed toward me and bent down to look me in the eye.

"What's wrong?" she asked

I replied by holding up a pencil. Followed by tears streaming down my face.

According to her, she was even more confused. I guess she expected that I was in physical pain. But I was not. And holding up a pencil made no sense.

But I was in pain. The teacher had cut the pencils in half and had given us each our half.

Eventually, as my mother tells the story, I hiccupped and asked how was I to write with such a small pencil. I asked for a whole pencil.

I am apt to believe my mother's tale as I strongly detest anything but a new well-sharpened no. 2 pencil.

So, you see, words have long mattered to me. And they matter to me for lots of reasons. Words matter to me in my capacity as an academic, but more importantly, they matter because of the connection I have to words, a connection that makes me feel loved and secure. So not writing was a profound loss and symptomatic of the fact that I was trying to survive in what, for me, was a very violent space.

Eventually, I exited that place that encapsulated so much of my pain. But one does not exit such a space without wounds and deep wounds. I had endured for ten long years. And those ten years were present on my mind, my body, and my spirit. During that period, I began to associate with violence, harm, and torment. And so, I retreated into me. Eventually, I would find therapists, Black therapists, that understood the violence associated with racism and how Black women experience such violence. They offered me the help I needed to gain perspective on all that I was trying to desperately manage—the swamp. I found Black therapists who heard me, saw me, and held the space I needed by giving me a language to express my experiences with race-gender violence. These therapists invited me back into my feeling body. They told me I was suffering from race-based trauma and resulting posttraumatic stress disorder (PTSD).

PTSD

It still seems so foreign when I think or speak of PTSD. The acronym does not easily slide off my tongue. But I try to make it real so as not to be consumed by it all. And so, I fought—weekly therapy sessions, journaling, yoga, speaking—telling my story of race-gender violence, resisting, and, more importantly, finding a way to live with it all. I had to find a way to feel and live my truth despite my experiences with race-gender violence. It was not easy then, and it's not easy now. But,

I entered
a journey from trauma,
to now learning to live with trauma.
I called on "the Black mother within each of us"[12]
And entered into
A sensual, spiritual, and political project of self-recognition
and self-actualization.
Entering into that space,
that space that anchors me/us against oppression.
Opening me/us up to "the affirmation of the particulars of
[our] lived experiences"[13]
I found my way
to my erotic.

Entering into my erotic has been and is a process. A process of deep joy, pain, self-reflection, and learning how to be in community. I have had deep conversations with myself about what it means to be a Black woman, a citizen of a previous British colony who migrated to the US at the age of sixteen, who mothers, who is a professor, who was once married, about how I engage in capitalism, my work, Christianity, and life in general. As part of my process of entering my erotic, I read a lot of the words of Black women and use these words to ask myself to think critically of how I engage in work.

"Within the celebration of the erotic in all our endeavors, my work becomes a conscious decision—a longed for bed which I enter gratefully and from which I rise up empowered." (Lorde 1984, 55) I wanted my work and not just my work in a capitalist sense, but my being, my "aesthetics of existence" that Toni Cade Bambara (1983) talks about, to allow me to rise up feeling empowered. I wanted the words, my writing, to deeply reflect my interior, that place of truth.

> *Why? Because*
> *our definition of self*
> *is sharpened*
> "by exposing the self in work."[14]
> *The act of self-definition*
> is a part,
> *a crucial part,*
> of the liberating practice that is central to Black feminism.[15]

I did not simply want to write about Black feminism. I wanted to practice Black feminism.

I did not simply want to write about Black feminine self-articulation. I wanted to practice Black feminine self-articulation.

I did not simply want to write about freedom and Black women's freedom. I wanted to practice freedom.

I wanted all of me to be reflected in all I do.

I wanted to be "wild" in all I do. I wanted to create me in my truth and have it underlie all I do. This, to me, was how I would approach race-gender violence and the resulting trauma. I long for all of this even in a context where "the opportunities for Black women to carry out autonomously defined investigations of self in a society which through racial, sexual and class oppression systematically denies our existence have been by definition limited" (Hull and Smith 1982, xviii). Writing became my way of living—for carrying out my investigations of self.

I cannot pinpoint the turning point at which I was able to come back to writing. I thought my days of writing were long behind me. And to some extent, that is true. The nature and being of my writing have changed. My sense of myself as a writer has changed. How I practice writing has changed. And I cannot always speak to these changes in a tangible manner, and I have come to accept that what rests on the interior need not always be defined tangibly. But the things I have written since exiting that space and being diagnosed with PTSD seem different—the style, the organization, the tone, and tenor of it all is different. I can tell you that once I had a language of what I was experiencing—race-gender violence and PTSD—I had to find a way to express it all.

Tamika Carey's analysis of Black women writers, expresses how writing becomes that conduit that affords Black women with maps, imaginative maps, to healing and as a source for writing oneself free. Through writing, I was able to "enact [my] agency in resisting or repairing the conditions that wound" me (Carey 2016, 27). *Erotic Testimonies* is, in part, my testimony of how I put all of the pieces of me back together in the face of race-gender violence. It is a spiritual, sensuous, and political project that seeks to see Black women and our truths.

Truth Telling: Black Feminism and Poetic Inquiry

epistemology creates the methodology
as methods have politics.[16]
i lay bare my politics.
a politics
resting in and birthed from
my experiences,
the experiences of those who came before me
and the experiences of those who will come after.
a politics of truth-telling.
these are mine.

Erotic Testimonies: Black Women Daring to Be Wild and Free is a Black feminist autoethnographic, ethnographic, poetic inquiry study of Black women's interior. I rely on Black feminist theory because,

"Unlike any other movement
Black feminism provides the theory."
A theory that
"clarifies the nature of black women's experience."[17]
For me, it is
a theory of resistance.[18]
A theory and a way of being that allows me/us
to challenge
narratives of Black female inferiority.
Exposing the cracks in movements that
see only race or gender and not both,[19]

and to resists the marginalization of Black women.
Allowing me/us
to talk back[20]
Making #BlackGirlMagic,
which is "a form of critical literacy used by
Black femmes, girls, and women,
to invent and/or imagine themselves in a society,"[21]
that often fails to see their personhood.

I use Black feminism as a theory and a "method." Black feminism speaks to the value of storytelling as a means of understanding the positionality of Black women. As April Baker-Bell (2017) asserts,

> Black feminist–womanist storytelling is a methodology that weaves together autoethnography, the African American female language and literacy tradition, Black feminist/womanist theories, and storytelling to create an approach that provides Black women with a method for *collecting* our stories, *writing* our stories, *analyzing* our stories, and *theorizing* our stories at the same time as *healing* from them. (531, emphasis in original)

Black feminism offers me a praxis of doing research. In a speech I gave in March 2019 at the University of Southern California, Los Angeles, I spoke of doing research as dwelling in the space between the knowing-not knowing-unknowing. That is the space that allows for creativity and, more importantly, for truth-telling. Dwelling in this space, which I identify as part of my praxis of Black feminism, makes me pause before undertaking a project. For example, it has led me not to use the term research but instead think of what I engage in as storytelling—which is better aligned with the Black feminine energy that undergirds my sense of self. I came to this through one of the central principles of Black feminism: reflexivity. Storytelling, to me, suggests engagement, a flow between the teller and listener. And these roles are dynamic as the teller needs to listen as much as the listener, and the listener "talks back" to the storyteller as much as the storyteller is talking to the listener. This brings me to a second underlying principle of Black feminism, which suggests a connectedness and resulting responsibility experienced by Black women (see Collins 2000). This is not to suggest that Black feminism does not recognize the uniqueness of individual Black women, but instead, it suggests that there is a "link between African American women's experiences as a heterogeneous collectivity and resulting group knowledge" (Taylor 2005, 1475).

Additionally, Black feminism offers me the approach of Black feminist autoethnography.

> *Autoethnography calls for us*
> "because of what we have learned.
> to reflect on what could be different."[22]
> *Black feminist autoethnography*
> *holds the potential to promote change.*
> *Calling me/you/us*
> "to raise social consciousness."
> *of the everyday Black woman and her struggles*
> *that result from*
> *the intersecting oppressions we face.*
> *Allowing my/your/our knowledge to*
> "be labeled, acknowledged, and remembered as [we] wish.[23]
> *Resisting those*
> "controlling images"[24]
> *allowing us the opportunity*
> *to tell our stories*
> *and,*
> *from our*
> *standpoint. Humanizing us.*
> Black feminist autoethnography // calls.

Blended in with Black feminism and Black feminist autoethnography is poetic inquiry. Poetic inquiry is a way of not only reading and presenting the existing literature but also presenting the testimonies of the women who inform this text. Monica Prendergast (2006, 369) suggests that poetic inquiry can serve as "an alternative method for understanding and representing key theories and texts." Prendergast (2006) offers the following process of engaging in poetic inquiry:

> All the words in these poems are to be found where cited in the original source texts. I have played with line breaks, patterns on the page, parentheses, and the occasional use

> of repetition for emphases. This present work is an attempt to capture a number of different, and valuable, voices and theoretical perspectives through the crystallizing and creative process of found poetry. (372)

Erotic Testimonies brings together all of me. I opted not to fragment the pieces of me, which blend to influence my experiences as a Black woman, my truth. To do such could result in my failing to practice and make real my aesthetic of self. Through my experiences as a Black woman, I have

> learned that if I didn't define myself for myself, I would be crunched into other people's fantasies for me and eaten alive. My poetry, my life, my work, my energies for struggle were not acceptable unless I pretended to match somebody else's norm. I learned that not only couldn't I succeed at that game, but the energy needed for that masquerade would be lost to my work. (Lorde 1984, 137)

Simply put, I wanted my energy not to be lost. And so, I honor that in the way I tell the story of Black women who engage their erotic.

Black Feminine Interiority: A Portal into the Erotic and Deep Feelings

While always linked to the material world and its attendant realities, the interior, as Kevin Quashie (2012, 6) notes, is not only a bulwark "against dominance of the social world," but interiority "has its own sovereignty." Black women often have knowledge that rests in the interior—a sovereign knowledge. It is ever-present; it is based on the past and looks to the future. It is that knowledge that Lorde speaks to and about when discussing how to use the erotic and the feelings that we access when we enter into and use our erotic.

It is often argued that Black women produce knowledge and wisdom based on their lived experiences and the generational modes and methods of surviving duress that results from multiple and interlocking forms of oppression. As Tamara Beauboeuf-LaFontant (2002, 72) states, "Because so many black women have experienced the convergence of racism, sexism, and classism, they often have a particular vantage point on what constitutes evidence . . . valid action . . . and morality." In speaking on Black women's literacies, Elaine Richardson (2002, 680) assert that literacies are "the development of skills . . . that help females advance and protect themselves and their loved ones in society." These skills involve the "social practices that influence the ways [Black women] make meaning and assert themselves socio-politically in subordinate as well as official contexts" (Richardson 2002, 680).

At times that knowledge is kept in the interior of Black women's consciousness. Joan Morgan (2015) explores the notion of "Black female interiority" in their work that explores Black women and the erotic, sexuality, and pleasure.

> Black female interiority is
> "the quiet composite of mental, spiritual and psychological
> expression
> encompassing
> the broad range of feelings, desires, yearning"
> *that are often held private and secret*
> *because of*
> "the politics of silence"[25]
> *that we are often introduced too early in our girlhood lives.*

Black female interiority is also thought of as embodying "the codicil to cultural dissemblance." (Morgan 2015, 37) The notion of dissemblance is, in part, drawn from the work of Darlene Clarke Hine who also speaks on the interiority of Black women, specifically those who experienced assault and harassment in the workplace. Clark Hine understands dissemblance as the secrecy that surrounds Black women's sexuality. Interiority is what happens in "the face of the pervasive stereotypes and negative estimations of the sexuality of black women," which results in Black women "collectively creat[ing] alternative self-images" to "shield from scrutiny these private, empowering definitions of self" (Clarke Hine1995, 380–87). In *Erotic Testimonies*, Black women's interiority is understood as that internal sovereign consciousness that is intergenerational, historical, and contemporary. It is that place where feelings reside, the place of truth, that allows us to seek a sovereign Black feminine personhood. Black women's interiority offers an understanding of a freedom that allows them to transcend multiple oppressions and to live their erotic—their truths.

Woven Conversation

Erotic Testimonies shows us that living the erotic is an active process that is fluid, filled with ritual, silence, and contemplation. My recitation of the names of Black women lost to us because of state-sanctioned violence, which I shared in the prelude to this introductory chapter, is but one example of how Black women engage the erotic. In part, this work is my story mingled with the stories of four Black women whom I have witnessed their testimony of living their erotic. They have their own independent and intertwined testimonies. The testimonies I now weave together to create a whole, recognizing that pieces are missing in a manner reminiscent of my grandmother's testimonies.

In this chapter, "Testifying," I offered the reader a guide for understanding the erotic and Black women's interior. This introductory chapter situates me, the "researcher" in this project, by relying on autoethnography to tell the story of what drew me to Audre Lorde's "Uses of the Erotic: The Erotic as Power." It is important to speak to how, as a Black woman in the academy, I have had to work in a context of race-gender violence and how I was able to find a place where my work felt like it was my truth—allowing me to exist in a place of wholeness—what I refer to as my sacred self. When I dwell in this sacred self, I experience freedom. This chapter also serves as a guide for reading the subsequent chapters by articulating the mixed approach that relies on Black feminism, autoethnography, ethnography, and poetic inquiry. I bring together these theories and approaches to invite you, the reader, to walk with the testimonies shared in this project.

Chapter 2, "Oh, Isn't It Wild?"[26] brings us a little deeper into my imagination of what it means to be a Black woman who dares to live wild and free. I rely on music, Janet Jackson's song "Control," for example, to think of how Black women are expected to walk particular lines. These lines result from race and gender and how they are intertwined to create a context where being wild is frowned upon by some, and consequently, our sense of freedom is limited. Beyond this, the chapter gets into the notion of self-identification, a process that Audre Lorde suggests we must engage in if we are to live our erotic, thereby allowing ourselves to feel/experience freedom. A word of caution. I am not necessarily concerned with formulating a "definition" of a wild Black woman. Thus, this chapter should not be read as such. I write in this chapter that when Black women choose to be wild, they choose their understanding of being wild; they are trusting, and deeply, their feelings. As you engage this chapter, maybe you interchange your song, or reading, or what I call your sacred text, to formulate your understanding of being wild as a way of thinking with us. I recognize that this is not what is typically expected of academic books. We are often required to offer concrete definitions that allow for measurement and testing, but that is not what this book is about. As I write, Black women have a way of knowing, and it is not always captured in social scientific methods/methodologies. The same methods/methodologies often do not see Black women. And I want to honor Black women's ways of knowing (I talk more about this in the conclusion).

Chapters 3 through 6 offer the testimonies of the women. I start in chapter 3 with Maya's testimony, "I want to Be Totally Free." Chapter 4, "It's Just Easier to Fuck," holds Sekile's testimony, and in chapter 5, you find Val's story, "A Barefoot Girl Howling at the Moon." "Since I Am Divine and I Am Feminine, It Is All Me," chapter 6, is Lakeesha's testimony. The individual chapters capture what Lorde speaks about when she writes of her engagement with the erotic. This includes, as she writes, "sharing of joy," "the open and fearless underlining of my capacity for joy," "it feels right to me," and "sharing deeply any pursuit with another person."

Chapter 7, "Talking to the Sugar Canes," explores Black women's "capacity for feeling" and all that we feel. This includes feelings of joy, sorrow, anger, mourning, and truth. Using the testimonies shared by the women who inform *Erotic Testimonies*, alongside my story and my gran's testimony, I explore how self-identified Black women embrace their capacity for feeling—thereby living their erotic.

Chapter 2

Oh! Isn't It Wild?[1]

Prelude II

> Girl, bring yuh wild behind inside.
> She too wild for me!
> Don't be like dem wild ass women.
> Sit your wild behind down.
> Girl, wah yuh doin' wid dat wild ting pon top yuh head?
> . . .

How often do Black femmes, girls, and women encounter any of the above statements? I do not have scientific data, but when I ask Black women if they have been on the receiving end of any of the above statements, have heard any of the utterances, or have even deployed one themselves, inevitably, they all nod. "Wild" follows Black women through our life cycle. In so many ways, we have been told that we are wild, not to be wild, that our hair is wild, and that, in essence, being wild is bad. As Toni Morrison (1992, 165) writes, "A wild woman is the worst of all. So, the warnings the girls got were part of a whole group of things to look out for lest the baby come here craving or favoring the mother's distraction." Like so many narratives directed at Black femmes, girls, and women, wild is constructed as bad. And something to avoid, and as Morrison suggests, it can travel through one's lineage. To be wild is to be nonprototypical and nonconformist. To be wild is to be forced to the margins of society. To be wild is to not color inside the lines. Or so they tell us.

I often make fun and say that while I have earned a PhD I have yet to learn how to color inside the lines. My inability or unwillingness to color inside the lines has been met with resistance—resistance both inside and outside of me. At times it is just hard being a Black girl/woman and not have to confront what it means to be "prototypical," to color inside the lines, especially when we are told in so many ways over our life cycle that being "wild" is bad. And yet, here I am writing about wild women, and not just any wild women, but Black wild women.

~

I was fifteen when Janet Jackson's album *Control* came out. I was in my last year of secondary school and had decided that I had done what I needed to do there. It made better sense for me not to return for an additional year. Instead, I would start college. Control—that is what Janet sang about. She told us how she wanted to be called "Ms. Jackson—if you nasty." Why? Because she was in control. I, like Janet, wanted to be in control of my education and what I pursued. I was so young to think that I could.

In my last term, I was actively engaged in raising money for our graduation ceremony—the first of its kind at my high school. I approached nightclubs and asked them to let us host parties and split the proceeds from the door. I organized variety shows and held them at the end of the school day. We performed a dance to Janet Jackson's "Control" at one such show. We strutted onto the stage, got in formation long before Beyoncé made it into an anthem, and waited for the curtain to rise. The music started, and we commenced our routine.

"I'm in control," Janet declared.

Yeah, I called her Janet in my imagination. She was the only Black girl somewhat close to my age that I had seen on television. And so, in my imagination, we had grown up together; thus, calling her Janet made sense to me. Dancing to that song "Control" had so many meanings to me as a teenager. I can remember how the lyrics resonated. I can remember feeling free.

We raised the money for the graduation. Fifteen going on sixteen, that's how old I was at that time.

Control

Growing up in Barbados, there was not much room for a Black girl to engage in self-articulation, the type of self-articulation expressed by Janet across the nine songs that compile that album. The self-articulation I expressed when I decided not to return to high school was not always accepted. I was considered wild. The lines of demarcation were always pretty clear. It was a demarcation of wild versus nonwild. The categorization of being wild was accompanied by a type of punishment—social, cultural, and even physical.

Parents and institutions often worked hard to ensure that their daughters/girls would not be considered "wild." I remember when a young lady in my class became pregnant. Of course, that was scandalous; it was the 1980s, and notions of purity were dominant (and still are to this day). The power structure of the school decided, given her fracture of what was proper, how dare she at that age become pregnant, not to allow her to return to school after the birth of her child. I remember how angry my mother was at that decision. And as such, her protest of the decision was no surprise. My parents were actively involved in the parent association, and what I know is that there was a meeting and that the young woman returned to school the following year. We never openly talked about what happened. I was proud of my mother for fighting for this young woman to return to school. But it was also a moment of contradiction for me. Sex and sexuality were not necessarily openly discussed in my house—mainly, we never discussed me as a sexual being. Do not get me wrong, my mother did not shy away from being open about sex and sexuality, but there was no space to discuss me in all of it—thus, the contradiction.

So, imagine what it felt like to be fifteen, going on sixteen and listening to Ms. Jackson—"if you nasty"—and grappling with the notion of control. My parents allowed me some latitude of self-articulation, but I had to stay within the lines. For example, they allowed me to opt to go to a Pentecostal church when I was about nine years old (neither of my parents was/is Pentecostal, and at that time, they were not active churchgoers). They allowed me to determine not to return to school and start college. But I cannot claim that I was totally free of not having to conform to the expectations, implicit and explicit, of not being a nonwild girl (here I go breaking the rules of the English language—I may do that from time to time in this book). While I will not collapse differences between Barbados and the United States, I suggest that respectability politics (see Cooper 2018; Higginbotham 1992) is prevalent in both spaces. I can distinctly remember being told, "Don't make us shame," as I departed Barbados for college. Don't make us shame required no explanation—I knew it meant not to go and behave wild and, God forbid, become a pregnant unwed "girl." And it also meant that I should not bring shame, via my behaviors, to the island of Barbados. I needed to engage in respectability politics is the message I was sent.

In *Zami: A New Spelling of My Name*, Audre Lorde explores the structures of authority that exist in Caribbean homes. She shows how these structures of authority are malleable, crossing boundaries, spaces, and time, and how they are used to control one's imagination of self. In response to these structures of authority, Lorde (1982) writes,

> learn isn't the right word to use for my beginning to talk, because to this day, I don't know if I didn't talk earlier because I didn't know how, or if I didn't talk because I had nothing to say that I would be allowed to say without punishment. Self-preservation starts very early in West Indian families. (21–22)

Silence became her mode of protection—a tactic she used to protect herself from punishment. In *Zami* Lorde also shows the various structures of authority outside of the home that were deployed in attempts to "contain" her wildness. One poignant story she shares is the tale of writing her name. Keep in mind that Lorde was nearsighted, and she was a very young child who received the disciplining technique that she recalls. This was a kindergarten classroom (I quote at length).

> I printed my best AUDRE. I had never been too good at keeping between straight lines no matter what their width, so it slanted down across the page something like this:
>
> A
>
>   U
>
>   D
>
>   R
>
>   E
>
> The notebooks were short, and there was no more room for anything else on that page. So I turned the page over, and wrote again, earnestly and laboriously, biting my lip,

L

O

R

D

E

half-showing off, half-eager to please.

The teacher's response:

> "You don't even want to try and do as you are told." "Imagine that, a big girl like you. Such a shame, I'll have to tell your mother that you won't even try. And such a big girl like you!" Yet the teacher does not frame this situation as something that can be isolated and addressed individually. "Now you copy that letter exactly the way it is, and the rest of the class will have to wait for you." (Lorde 1982, 25–26)

Control

At really young ages, in our families and in the structures we encounter, Black girls are subjected to systems of control. To protect us, limit us, for whatever reason—we are subjected to control. Black femmes, girls, and women are structured to color in the lines.

LINES

In 1985 Janet Jackson gave me another view into the notion of control.

I stood on the stage, waiting for the beat to drop, waiting for that first line to play. I hummed in anticipation,

This is a story about control/
And this time I'm gonna do it my way

"Control" and *Zami*, Black women's projects of self-articulation, gave this Black girl and now woman (I would read *Zami* much later in life) a sign-post of what it meant to be wild, a wild Black girl/woman. Both offered me their testimony so that I could find my way to my testimony—which for me is a form of self-articulation.

Signposts: How Black Women Dare to Be Wild

"Thus, public citizenship and private self-making, or the process by which individuals come to know themselves within competing systems of control, have long been in discord for Black women" (Jackson, 2020, 108). This notion of discord is often discussed among Black women, rather openly or implicitly; we see much of this in Black feminist literature and theorizing.

Control is often talked about as controlling images,[2]
As scripts written on Black women's Bodies,[3]
That politics of disgust[4]
that results in Black women's invisibility or hypervisibility.
Stigmatizing.
Punishing.
So, sometimes we get silent.
Not always knowing from whence silence comes.
Is it that we have nothing to say?
Or is it that we are seeking to protect ourselves?
Regardless,
we become shadow bodies.
"Ass and strong woman scripts,"
Seen but not seen[5]
Shadows
Existing in that "space in-between—a space of both proximity and separation,"[6]
We experience the "dislocation of body and voice."[7]
But we are brave,[8] *at least some of us,*
and seek to create space.
Telling our own stories.
Controlling narratives, our own.
Daring to live wild and free.

We take control by engaging in self-articulation and self-valuation. Often writing and imagining ourselves into existence by critiquing the structures—out-group and in-group—that limit our possibilities to be whole and recipients of justice and equity. Black feminists and critical scholars posit that Black women are often the recipients of social power that is executed and negotiated via the use of language, narratives, and representations; that is, images, myths, and icons (see Jordan-Zachery 2017; Collins 2000; Morrison 1992). In *Shadow Bodies*, I engage the notion of scripting, understood as "the process of the transformation of the body into discursive text, to which signs and stereotypes can then be applied for the purpose of assigning meaning," to show how the intragroup performance of intersectionality positions some Black women not to be seen and in essence to be controlled (Jordan-Zachery 2017, 54). Through scripting, the Black female body becomes the discursive text written on and read to control Black women (see Guy-Sheftall 2002; Roberts 1997). Thus, it is no surprise that Black women will seek to control their bodies—to be in control via the politics and practice of self-articulation—all as a form of testimony. Testify, that is what Black women do, to make themselves visible, to assert their control. They testify like the women who sat in the pews of Welchman Hall Church of God (see chapter 1).

Stretching lines
to make space.
That's why we testify.
Resisting boundaries of invisibility and hypervisibility,[9]
agentic strategy.
Reimagining and remaking "liminal space of alterity."[10]
Learning how to perch outside and inside.[11]

As part of their response to race-gender oppression, of which class and sexuality are intimately connected, Black women have sought to create space. This space is used to express their identity, creativity, and visions of justice and freedom. The space is necessary to live their truths. By making space, Black women challenge liberal democratic capitalist ideologies by inserting themselves into the conversation as a form of critique and as a form of imagining a new democratic practice. In *Black Girl Magic Beyond the Hashtag*, we talk about the labor involved in Black women's practices of self-articulation (Jordan-Zachery and Harris 2019). And yes, it is labor. We see examples of this labor in the works of Audre Lorde, bell hooks, Toni Morrison, Ntozake Shange, and Paule Marshall, among many more. This is the type of work I have engaged, to enter into my erotic, to make myself whole.

~

> Everything I've ever done, in the writing world, has been to expand articulation rather than to close it.
>
> —Toni Morrison, "The Salon Interview—Toni Morrison" (Jaffrey 1998)

> You have to be clever to figure out how to be welcoming and defensive at the same time. When to love something and when to quit. If you don't know how, you can end up out of control or controlled by some outside thing.
>
> —Toni Morrison, *Jazz*, 9

> i found god in myself and i loved her
> i loved her fiercely
>
> —Ntozake Shange, *For Colored Girls Who Have Considered Suicide/When the Rainbow Is Enuf*, 63

Black women, like Toni Morrison, Alice Walker, Ntozake Shange, and Janet Jackson, work to control their narratives which allows them, and us, to "scrutinize all aspects of our existence." (Lorde 1984, 57). *This has resulted in Black women thinking critically on how to use their anger. As Audre Lorde asserted,* "My anger has meant pain to me, but it has also meant survival, and before I give it up I'm going to be sure that there is something at least as powerful to replace it on the road to clarity" (Lorde 1984, 132). And so we see Black feminists, such as Brittney Cooper in *Eloquent Rage* (2018), and Rachel Griffin in "I AM an Angry Black Woman" (2012), claiming their right to be angry. According to Cooper, an expression of rage is, in essence, a defiance of the practice of respectability politics. Respectability politics is thought of as being "predicated on extremely conservative ideas about what a proper race man and a proper race woman are and should look like" (Cooper 2018, 55). Individuals practice respectability politics in hopes "that Black people can overcome many of the everyday, acute impacts of racism by dressing properly and having education and social comportment [which] is, first and foremost, performed as a kind of sartorial prerogative" (Cooper 2018, 147). Cooper suggests that, in essence, respectability politics will not save the Black race and that it is a limiting performance of self—individually and collectively. Respectability politics is another line Black women are often asked to exist within. My testimony, in part, speaks to my relationship with respectability politics and how I was taught to be a "good" Black girl. However, my reality has shown me that adhering to the practice of respectability has never saved me from race-gender violence.

Those lines cannot protect me!

And so Black women resist by offering alternative testimonies to the notion of respectability. Black feminist writers and critical theorists, as part of the practice and politics of self-articulation, also write about Black women as *ratchet*. Ratchetness is considered as a practice and space for challenging and disrupting what is perceived as forced respectability (Meggs 2021; McEachern 2017; Pickens 2015; Cooper 2012). Ratchetness is offered as a cultural technique that is used to allow some to move through oppression via the celebration of creativity and individual expression. Ratchet, like Black Girl Magic, is a fraught term. Chie Davis (2014) and Janel George (2015), among others, suggest that ratchet works to demean Black women. This is how Black women, through contestation, work to expand self-articulations.

Magic and Black Girl Magic is also part of the practice and politics of Black women's self-articulation. While some credit, and rightly so, CaShawn Thompson, who tweets at @thepbg, with the hashtag #BlackGirlsAreMagic, the notion of Black feminine magic has been used by others prior to 2013. In 1983 the great literary artist Alice Walker wrote that (Black) women were "driven to a numb and bleeding madness by the springs of creativity in them for which there was no release, and I knew I did not want to be one of those women. They were creators who lived lives of spiritual waste" (233). Walker also suggested that despite race-gender-class oppressive structures, these same women "handed on the creative spark, the seed of a flower they themselves never hoped to see: or like a sealed letter they could not plainly read" (240). She further writes that Black women imagine and create a "universe in the image of her personal conception of Beauty . . . as if by magic" (241). What Walker suggests, in part, is that Black women work to manifest their visions of themselves, crafting an imagined understanding of themselves that is outside of the realm of the social, political, and economic control they often experience. Thompson and Walker use the concept of magic to describe the work done by Black women and how Black women articulate resistance to the invisibility/hypervisibility—cultural, political, and social—that they often face. Like the concept of ratchet, Black Girl Magic is contested. Linda Chavers (2016, n.p.) offers a critique of #BlackGirlMagic by suggesting that the notion of the magical Black woman erases the reality that Black girls are human.

There is a long and deep history of Black women engaging in the practice of self-articulation seeking to make visible the Black feminine divine. Self-articulations are used to foster diasporic activist networks that are "motivated by a shared desire to reconfigure unequal social structures, achieve sociopolitical recognition, and gain respect and unfettered access to the societal benefits of full citizenship" (Harrison 2019, 45). However, as Evelynn Hammonds (1994) reminds us, it is not enough to seek to simply respond to invisibility and silence because,

> in overturning the "politics of silence," the goal cannot be merely to be seen: visibility in and of itself does not erase a history of silence nor does it challenge the structure of power and domination, symbolic and material, that determines what can and cannot be seen. The goal should be to develop a "politics of articulation." This politics would build on the interrogation of what makes it possible for black women to speak and act. (141)

It is not enough to simply engage in self-articulation. We have to ensure that such articulations make space for the diversity of the Black feminine divine. Black women's self-articulation has to simultaneously recognize differences while not allowing those differences to become limitations. I argue that the women who share their testimonies in this book, because they are wild Black women, allow us a glimpse into how living beyond lines and limits may become a lived practice.

She Wild and It Makes Me Laugh

When I am asked, what is sometimes the dreaded question, what am I working on, and I say I'm working on a book on wild Black women, I tend to get a smirk. For the most part, individuals assume I am working on a book on socially defined promiscuous women. And then, when I dare mention the use of the erotic, eyebrows inevitably raise. Once I explain how I understand wild, there is often what feels like disappointment—oh, there is nothing tantalizing in the book is the unspoken response. But they do not fully understand what I mean by wild. In part because the notion of wild, in the context of gender and race, is a fraught concept.

> *Wild is part of Black women's* "oppositional gaze."[12]*/Wild doesn't just allow us to challenge understandings of Black womanhood, / Wild seeks to* "change reality"[13]*/Wild* "makes it possible for black women to speak and act."[14]*/Wild is a* "paradigm of growth."[15]*/Wild is* "personal liberation."[16]*/Wild is the embodied knowledge that lives*

Deep, in the feminine spiritual place
of the interior.
To be wild is to experience
freedom.

~

Black, Woman, and Wild don't go together
Or so I've been told

Kimberly Wallace-Sanders (2002, 2), in *Skin Deep, Spirit Strong*, writes that the Black female body has been socially constructed as wild. As she suggests, "the bodies of [B]lack women have not only been identified as erotic objects but have symbolized the most extreme sexuality imaginable: wild, insatiable, and deviant." To be perceived as wild is to be thought of as existing outside of the norms of society. To be wild is to not engage in respectability politics. To be wild is to not color inside the lines.

To be wild is to be
Unrestrained
Transitional
Traumatized
Untamed
Natural
Bisexual
Truthful
To be wild is to be outside the lines
Some mix dat with dat Blackness and you get
Welfare queen
Jezebel
Urban Teen Mother

Sapphire
Angry
Uppity
Slutty
Bitch
Wild connotes
Power

The controlling images, many of which are listed above, used to inform policy and the political treatment of Black women, hold at their core a particular and negative notion of wildness. A Eurocentric approach to interacting with what is perceived as wild is to "tame it" to "control" it. In the United States, social policy is but one tool used to control the perceived wild Black woman. This has given way to welfare reform of the 1990s (Jordan-Zachery 2009; Schram et al. 2009), to the criminalization and incarceration of Black women at disproportionate rates (The Sentencing Project 2020), to the expulsion of Black girls from K–12 schools at disproportionate and alarming rates (Morris 2016). Taming the perceived wild Black femme has also resulted in the silence around the murders of trans Black women (Letcher 2018). It has also produced silence around the disproportionate maternal mortality rates of Black women (Cooper Owens and Fett, 2019). The perceived wild Black femme, girl, and woman are controlled via multiple tactics across their lifespan.

So, how can I even begin to recover the wild Black woman? Or maybe the better question is, why would I want to recover something so fraught? As Patricia G. Lespinasse shows, the notion of the wild woman has informed several protagonists in various novels written by Black women. Lespinasse (2010) suggests that there are four wild archetypes.

1. Primitive Object: this wild woman is presented as coming from the earth or without origins; yet she is the original mother/wild woman figure even in the absence of children. As the original wild woman, she usually appears in the nude, with wild hair and other markers of natural beauty and power. An example of a Wild Woman as a primitive object is Wild in Toni Morrison's *Jazz*.

2. Spectacle: this particular wild woman is the object of the gaze. She usually appears as a songstress and uses the stage

as her platform even if she lacks an art form. She uses her instincts to guide and protect her interests. Her voice is both her sword and shield. An example of the wild woman as spectacle is Ursa Corregidora in Gayl Jones' *Corregidora* and Lutie Johnson in *The Street* by Ann Petry.

3. Licentious/Lesbian: this wild woman is morally and sexually unrestrained and unbound by societal norms. She often appears as bisexual or a lover of women. She is a transitional figure as she moves between her social world of moral codes and her secret world of dissent. She resists the boundaries associated with gender norms and other power structures that attempt to restrain her sexuality. An example of the Lesbian wild woman is Tante Atie in *Breath Eyes Memory* by Edwidge Danticat.
4. Mad woman: this wild woman has been traumatized to the point of madness. She might have Post-Traumatic Stress Disorder (PTSD—a disorder that can develop following a traumatic event that threatens your safety or makes you feel helpless) or exhibit symptoms of PTSD such as hallucinations and having no sense of time or reality. She is disconnected from her community because of her lack of association and often isolated because of language barriers. She is unable to express her emotions or the direct cause of her trauma. An example of the mad wild woman can be seen in the character portrayal of Martine Caco in *Breath Eyes Memory* by Edwidge Danticat and Pecóla Breedlove in Morrison's *The Bluest Eye* (14–15).

But there is one literary engagement with the wild Black woman that is particularly intriguing, and that is the one created by Toni Morrison in the novel *Jazz*. Why *Jazz*? Simply, the novel and the character resonate with me; maybe it has to do with the magical and complex way Morrison shapes her throughout the novel.

However, before I get to Wild, the character, I want to engage Ida Cox's famous song "Wild Women Don't Have the Blues." Black women in the blues tradition, such as Bessie Smith and Gertrude "Ma" Rainey, have boldly explored the notion of the wild woman in their music. But in thinking of the concept of the wild woman, Angela Davis (1998) writes,

"Ida Cox's 'Wild Women Don't Have the Blues' is among the most famous rendition of the portrayal of the nonconforming, independent woman." Furthermore, Davis argues that the "wild woman" personifies "the woman who consciously rejects mainstream values, especially that prescribing passivity in relations with men" (Davis 1998, 38–39) Consider that Ida Cox ([1924] 1981) recorded and sang this song in 1924; in her husky tone she sang,

> You never get nothing by being an angel child/
> You better change your ways and get real wild/. . .
> Wild women are the only kind that really get by.

Through her embodiment of the wild woman, Cox casts off the regulatory and performative functions of raced-heteronormativity, which suggest that a good woman's, and a good Black woman's, self-performance should be chaste and that she should engage in monogamy. Instead, Cox offers a different articulation of Black womanhood, one that brazenly represents her desires, and not just sexual desires, in a way that they cannot be ignored. Consider her song "One Hour Mama" (Cox and Grainger [1939] 1980), which not only offers a critique of men's sexual ability but offers the listener a celebration of her own sexual ability:

> I've always heard that haste makes waste . . .
> I'm a one hour mama,
> so no one minute papa.

Cox, it can be argued, sets the stage for Black women's sexual articulation telling us, in part, that she does not desire a man who cannot satisfy her. Years later, Beyoncé (2016) on the visual album *Lemonade*, in the song "Formation," sang, "When he fuck me good, I take his ass to Red Lobster. 'cause I slay." And then, in the midst of the COVID-19 pandemic, economic decline, and police/state-sanctioned murders of Black men and women, there was "WAP" (wet ass pussy) by Cardi B featuring Megan Thee Stallion. Two Black women rapping about wet ass pussy. Spitting the following bars:

> Put this pussy right in your face . . .
> This pussy is wet, come take a dive.

Testify! I thought when I first heard this song. It took me back to Cox's singing which was a testimony of naming desires.

That's what Black women are doing. They are testifying.

But some do not know how to hold space for Black women's testimony. They cannot see Black women. WAP is responded to as a homage to (Black) women's sexuality or as vulgar and warranting censorship. Some appear shocked that Black women can even sing or express their sexual desires, or god forbid, have the audacity to state what pleases them. I laughed when I read some of the responses to WAP. I thought, have you been paying attention to Black women? And I wondered, have they ever listened to or read Black women's testimonies? There is much chatter on social media platforms, like Twitter, with hashtags such as #listentoBlackwomen.

But here is what I have noticed with the calls to listen to Black women. These calls are less about the needs of Black women and more about how Black women will save society. And Black women have "clapped back" by reminding folk that Black women's labor should be in service of themselves (Jordan-Zachery and Alexander-Floyd 2019).

Black women are often expected to perform in a particular way, and so when Cardi B and Megan Thee Stallion dropped "WAP," it went against some people's understandings of what it means to be a non-wild Black woman. Some were seemingly shocked by the bravado of their sexual powers and their expressions of how they experience sexual pleasure (not to suggest that the song mimics either Cardi B or Megan Thee Stallion's lived realities). Why? Because they do not really listen to Black women. Had they been listening to Black women, they would have known that Cardi B and Megan Thee Stallion were continuing the tradition of Ma Rainey, who sang, "Went out last night with a crowd of my friends They must've been women, 'cause I don't like no men." Maybe, had they listened to Donna Summer's "Love to Love You Baby" (original extended version, Oasis Records 1975) where she just moans in ecstasy, they would not have been stunned. Sometimes we just moan, which is our testimony, but that can go unheard.

Moaning.
Riding.
Speakin'.
Telling men to Lick it before you stick it[17]

And women just to lick it 'cause they can't stick it
Black Women and sexual pleasure
Homage versus vulgar
Stereotypes have us caught in a binary
"ranging from our uniquely mammified asexuality
to our naturally
animalistic,
wanton
and
licentious ways."[18]
Saying #ListentoBlackwomen
Yet, never really hearing our moans as we speak our truths.
Seeking to use our erotic.
And exercising control.
Power.

Narratives on Black women's pleasure—and sexual pleasure—are often dismissed through narratives of legitimacy and wildness. The essence of these narratives, singularly and combined, suggests that a "good" Black girl doesn't behave in certain ways. *Don't be like that wild ass woman* is but one way that is sometimes conveyed. Yet, Black women have not shied away from expressing their sexual desires even when it seemingly contradicts respectability politics. But when some seek to treat Black women's sexuality and sexual pleasure in only one way, they are missing much of what Black women are actually testifying about. Black women are testifying about control.

It's more than sex/sexuality.

Enter *Pussy Prayers* (2018) by Black Girl Bliss. The title makes some gasp, and they wonder why I have this book just lying around my living room. After all, the word *pussy* carries a sense of salaciousness, and what "good" Black woman would display such a book is often the spoken and unspoken response. Like the term *wild*, pussy carries pejorative meanings that often require secrecy and keeping our desires and feelings in the interior. But Black Girl Bliss (2018) writes

> *Pussy*. This is the term I will be using to refer to the **creative** space between your thighs. . . . I like using the word pussy. Why? Because it's a "bad" word. It's irreverent, It's "unladylike." It's shocking. But the use of the word pussy is not vulgarity for

> vulgarity's sake. Words we've been taught are bad or naughty or nasty are usually words that carry tremendous *power*. (9, emphasis added)

Sex, pussy, wild . . . all words used sometimes to control the imaginations and options of Black femmes, girls, and women. Taking us outside of our erotic as they tend to police some feelings. So how can Black women experience control and express their creativity? More specifically, how can they resist these limiting structures to live their erotic? Allow me to turn to Wild, a character in Toni Morrison's *Jazz* (1992).

~

To be wild is to be true,
'cause being wild takes us from object to subject.

What does it mean for Black women to be a subject? In the foreword to *Jazz*, Toni Morrison (1992, xviii) writes that primary among the features of jazz, the music genre, is "inventions. . . . Improvisation, originality, change." In the novel, Wild embodies inventions, she is improvisation, she is original, and she signals change. Some who encounter Wild characterize her as "a naked berry-black woman . . . covered with mud and [with] leaves in her hair" who is living "among the trees" in that place "where wild women grow" (Morrison 1992, 144, 171, 177). This is the primitive archetype as discussed by Lespinasse (2010). Wild is also thought of as violent where "everything about her is violent" (Morrison 1992, 153). Again, we see the mad woman archetype (Lespinasse 2010). Wild is a dark-skinned woman who is thought of as a force who roams and wanders through the woods. She is often present but never indeed fully seen. Yet, those who interact with her know and feel her presence. Wild is mystery, an improvisation—never truly appearing in the same form and iteration. Wild embodies innovation—of thought and being. Wild is a mother who refuses the expectations of motherhood. She opts not to stay and raise her child; instead, she wanders.

In writing on the character Wild, Diakantoniou (2018) suggests that

> Wild is literally "the name of the sound." This is the model for *freedom* that Morrison is endorsing, as Wild manages to circumvent the control of any location . . . Wild creates her

> own, leaving traces upon which others stumble. Hence, Wild's indeterminacy, suggested also by the instability of her signification, allows her to practice a natural and beneficial form of track-making. Society is frightened by Wild because they do not understand her; her *rogue existence is not an accepted option for women.* (n.p., emphasis added)

In *Jazz*, the character Wild embodies freedom and truth she creates herself. Wild lives within her erotic. Wild moves from object to subject by living her truth. Toni Morrison's Wild informs much of my understanding of a Black wild woman. And in part, the character shows us how to see Black women. She does what Ma Rainey did in the famous song "Wild Women Don't Get the Blues," what Beyoncé did in her song "Formation," by telling us that she will decide if the sex was good. In *Erotic Testimonies*, we see what it means for a woman to talk about her "wet ass pussy"—that is, to name herself for herself. Morrison, through Wild, shows us that Black women's voices can be centered in the way that Donna Summer did when she just moaned. Black women have agency! And the way we have agency is to live our erotic—that is, our truths. And that sometimes requires us to be wild.

And so, as I think of Black wild women, I think of Wild. To be wild is to be the embodiment of a liberatory, Black feminist project as it involves moving beyond the gaze of white heteronormative, patriarchal, capitalist, sexist, racist, classist structures. And this is what Audre Lorde was speaking to when she encouraged us to engage in our erotic.

The Kernel

> That was a long and sometimes arduous journey toward self-possession. And that journey was sweetened by an increasing ability to stretch far beyond what I had previously thought possible—in understanding, in seeing common events in a new perspective, in trusting my own perceptions.
>
> —Audre Lorde, *Your Silence Will Not Protect You*, 35

When Black women choose to be wild, that is, when they choose their own understandings of being wild, they are trusting, and deeply, their feelings. These women recognize that they are not coloring within the lines, at least not always. But as Lorde suggests in the above quote, it is not an easy journey for Black women to achieve self-possession, the type of self-possession that Wild embodies. The "teacher" often stands over us, reminding us to write our names neatly within the lines. Once when I was in elementary school, my teacher chastised me about my handwriting. My response: I can pay attention to my thinking or my handwriting. I choose my thinking. I was ten. I did not stop to think of the repercussions of my response. And luckily for me, she allowed me to be. My handwriting has never truly improved, and I have long given up. This was not where I wanted to put my energy. It is like me, not exactly caring about literally coloring inside the lines. But I recognize that these relatively inconsequential actions do not exactly put me at risk. But they are necessary for the process and practice of self-articulation. These little acts are necessary for living in the erotic—that place of truth. These small acts are the kernel that Lorde talks about in the essay "Uses of the Erotic: The Erotic as Power." Sometimes that kernel needs to be massaged to help it form and take shape. Massaging sometimes requires us to resist and reject heteronormative, racist, patriarchal, and capitalist imaginations of what it means to be Black and woman. But as Audre Lorde warns, that can be feared—setting aside self-expectations can be a fearful endeavor.

That fear can stop us,
stop us from saying we don't want no one-minute man,
staying in relationships beyond their due dates,
working in jobs that are less than satisfying,
being unable to utter
Wet Ass Pussy,
because our tongues don't effortlessly glide over the word
pussy;
'cause pussy, like the erotic, becomes something used to shame,
to control,
to limit,
to force us into prescribed lines,
where we are monitored and told how to be.
Told not to be wild,
when wild is what we want to be,
so, we testify
we moan,

we cry out,
taking back control,
each little kernel of control
3
9
10
15
at each age
we massage, molding it all into
what we need it to be,
letting it sit, deep
deep in the interior,
that deep Black feminine space,
so that we can be
free
to one day become wild Black women.

Chapter 3

I Want to Be Totally Free

Maya's Testimony

Prelude III

I guess you can say that I came to Maya in my attempts to be stitched back together. I was looking for ways to heal from the race-gender violence I was experiencing. And by healing, I do not necessarily mean in a Western way that tends to center an individualistic approach, which tells one to change one's outlook. A health practitioner told me to simply "stop thinking about it." I wondered how that would change the fact that I am a Black woman who faces anti-Blackness, patriarchy, and sexism in the context of capitalism. When I explained the race-gender oppression I faced, I was once told by a therapist that she wished she could help me but didn't know how to and that if I could tell her what I needed, she would try to help. I never went back. And so, I sought ways to help me make it through, ways to be whole while being in community and resisting anti-Blackness. I eventually found Maya.

Consequently, when I think of Maya, I think of layers, patching, restoration, and a deep and complex journey into survival that gives way to rebirth. And as such, the title of her chapter, which is taken from her words and my experiences with her, is not surprising to me. At the end of our conversation, I asked her if there was anything that she wanted to share that we did not speak about. She mentioned her grandmother, Harriet Powers. Ms. Powers, an enslaved woman, was a quilter, and one of her quilts was displayed in the Smithsonian. It is believed that she was the first person to create a Bible quilt (see Moreno 2017). I think that this speaks to Maya's spirit, a willingness to chart her own path.

~

The first time I met Maya, I admit that I was suspicious. Here we were in the middle of what felt like nowhere, sitting on a yoga mat, gathered for a yoga retreat for women of color. She was/is the organizer. We gathered in a room for the opening ceremony. Eventually, Maya walked in. I thought to myself: How old is this woman, and what is she selling us? I guess you can say that I was not very trusting. But I sat, I listened, I danced, and I breathed. Eventually, Maya disclosed her age, and she shared a part of her healing/health journey with us. There was a collective gasp. She defied age and health. Slowly, my resistance ebbed into curiosity.

For two and a half days, I allowed myself to be curious, to lean into the space that Maya was curating. I allowed myself to feel. Eventually, Maya would be the one to train me to become a yoga teacher. I had been attending yoga classes, but it was Maya who truly introduced me to yoga and, particularly, sacred texts. As I went through my yoga training, Maya would teach me about the limbs of yoga with Svadhyaya: a study of the sacred scriptures and of one's self, being part of the second limb, Niyama (which loosely translates as "spiritual observances and self-discipline"). I can remember her telling me not to let anyone determine what is considered a sacred text for me, but instead that I should exercise agency in determining what I consider a sacred text. I had never thought of the writings of Black women as sacred texts. My yoga training allowed me to reimagine them. Trying to recover from race-gender trauma led me to collect Black women's writings and engage them in a different, sacred way. These sacred texts, which included works by the likes of Ruth King, bell hooks, Audre Lorde, and the words of my grandmother (although not written down), took on new meanings for me as they invited me to reimagine myself—to quilt me back together.

~

Maya feels filled with mystery and depth. Turquoise seems to fit beautifully with all that has been given to me by the ancestors regarding Maya. Consider that turquoise, a combination of blue and green, is associated with an "inward thinking person or highly intuitive" independent person who "often seek[s] fulfillment in a spiritual sense" (Color Psychology Meaning, n.d.) Thus, I'm not surprised that when I did as Audre Lorde instructed me, to let the ancestors guide the performative embodied reading, that turquoise and Yemayá, alongside the song "Window Seat," particularly the video, by Erykah Badu, were offered as the guides to the write up of Maya. They serve as the portals that allow me to engage in the dialectical process of testimony (see chapter 1). It is worth noting that Lorde channels the energies of African female Orishas, including Yemayá (Yemoja or Yemanjá, across many of her writings [see *Black Unicorn*], 1995). As Solimar Otero and Toyin Falola (2014, xviii) state, "Orisa-worshipping communities are sites where subjectivities are creatively produced within social and cultural contexts." Thus, it is not surprising that Lorde would channel Orishas in her writings. "From the House of Yemanjá" (1997, 6–7), Lorde writes that she is "the sun and the moon" and "the sharpened edge/ where day and night shall meet/ and not be/ one." In Lorde's use of Yemayá, she is presented as the archetypal Black mother, "the source of nourishment, the source of power for us all—black, white, male and female" (Kraft [1986] 2004, 147). And "the Black mother" is "that part of us which is chaotic, messy, deep, dark, ancient, old, and freeing" (147).

I was able to tap into a knowledge that guided me to Yemayá as a guide for Maya. Yemayá (Yemoja) is the Yoruba water deity, the guardian of the oceans and seas, and is considered the mother of all Orishas. Water is thought of as the life force, and as such, Yemayá is considered nurturing and maternal, and she is thought of as a healer as she has endured suffering. Furthermore, she is known for fiercely defending her children. Finally, Yemayá enjoys dancing (see Personal Introduction to Santeria n.d.).

Complex and defying boundaries, the giver of life, Yemayá seems to embody much of what I see and have experienced through and with Maya. And this is probably why I sense that Maya is filled with depth and mystery. One can sense a type of pain that led Maya to do the work she does and the underlying fierceness that seems to envelop her sense of protection and a desire that individuals be well and be treated well regardless of social location. In our songversation,[1] Maya said, "and when a Black woman is free of some of the things that challenge us, like drugs and alcohol and overeating and all that, that wisdom and that ability, the Black woman knowing it just blossoms." Part of her life's work is to help Black women blossom. In an interview with Susan Chaityn Lebovits (2010) for *Yoga Journal*, Maya stated, "I'm drawn to those who need yoga to help them change their lives after loss, grief, stress, or challenge."

And then there is Erykah Badu. Badu sings, "Can I get a window seat." This line/title suggests that she is not asking for permission to sit (on public transportation) but is operating from the position that access to the bus is hers, and she is simply asserting where she wants to sit. This may be read as a nod to the Civil Rights Movement of the 1960s that sought "access" to the bus. Also, it speaks to how Black women claim space and seek to be in public spaces. Additionally, "can I get a window seat" speaks to the duality of visibility/hypervisibility that many Black feminist theorists write about (Harris-Perry 2011; Guy-Sheftall 1995). Badu is inserting how she wants to be positioned, claiming power. Desire is also being expressed—how she wants to be seen. In writing about the significance of Badu (and Janelle Monáe), Nathalie Aghoro (2018, 330) says, "The continuous (re)naming and self-fashioning themselves represent deliberate acts of unmaking, remaking, and, ultimately, staging alternate ways of being in the world." In her song and the accompanying video, Badu is engaged in a politics and practice of staging an alternative Black womanhood. In the video, which resulted in a stir and ultimately Erykah Badu being fined for indecency, she strolls through the famous Dealey Plaza in Dallas, Texas, as she strips. This is the site of the assassination of President John F. Kennedy. And Badu inserts her Black woman self in this space as she discards each item of clothing while walking along the park. Her slow disrobement as she strolls through the park is not done in a sexualized matter. She does this in front of an unsuspecting audience without prior approval from the governing bodies. Towards the end of the video, we see "Evolved" tattooed across Erykah's back. As she approaches the site of Kennedy's assassination, we hear a single gunshot. Erykah lays naked and "assassinated," and the word "groupthink," written in blue letters, seems to erupt from her head, and the voice-over says, "They play it safe, are quick to assassinate what they do not understand . . . They are us. This is what we have become—afraid to respect the individual. A single personal event or circumstance can move one to change. To love herself. To evolve." I read this as her response to being told to color within the lines—to be confined by societal expectations of what it means to be simultaneously Black and woman. Badu resists containment of her wild Black woman self.

In addition to exploring how society can be limiting, Badu shows how she's exploring the interior when she sings, "Somebody say, 'Come back, come back baby, come back.' " I read this not necessarily as her yearning for someone external to ask her to come back. But she is looking, internally, for that "person," her truth, to bring her back to herself.

Lorde's "Uses of the Erotic," asks, how do we see ourselves? It calls on us to think of how we go into the interior to see what lies in each of us, our essence/feelings that make us who we are. And more importantly, Lorde invites us to think of how we come back to our truth in light of capitalist and patriarchal structures that tend to position us relative to production, where our value is measured in goods and services. The song's video picks up this type of questioning of societal structures. Badu, and similarly Maya, by bringing Black womanhood into this very white male space that dominates the US, asserts her autonomy and the right to control her body and how it is viewed and consumed.

Combined, turquoise, Yemayá, and "Window Seat" offer us a way of thinking with Maya's testimony. For one, Maya seems to sit "between," a blend that speaks to who she is. And this is captured in how she speaks to the colors she prefers. Take, for example, her use of coral which is neither pink nor orange, but between. I took it upon myself to look up the meaning of coral. It was suggested that coral does not conform. Instead, it challenges the norm. Second, Maya has a practice of healing, particularly through her use of yoga, and she bends notions of Black womanhood, not asking for permission to be seen or how to be seen.

September 22, 2020. At 2 p.m., we enter our Zoom conversation, or as India.Arie says, our "songversation" as it feels like more than just a conversation. The lyric and the laughter of it all envelopes me. I find myself leaning into the screen, the distance between us disappearing. The flatness of the monitor dissolves as we meet in time and space, creating an atmosphere of inquisitiveness, revelation, and discovery. I invite you into our "songversation."

I Still Consider Myself Wild

I asked, "What comes to mind when you hear the word wild?" There was a pause, a smile, and then laughter. The laughter was rich and deep, as though it held secrets and secrets only Maya could tell. I sat in my pew, waiting for the testimony that would come forth. Here is the testimony.

I still consider myself wild. I think when I was younger, I was wild in the truest sense, you know, where, where I really wanted to have adventures and do things that I wanted to do *only* because I wanted to do them, not because someone told me or said it would be fun. It's like I want to know what that's like. And so, I think I had a wild way of being and speaking.

My grandmother used to tell me, because I had such a fresh mouth, she'd say, she used to say, taste your words, sister, taste your words. And that serves me well today. I haven't had a job with an organization in over [*trails off*]. I can't tell you how many years. I've always worked for myself. So, it's wild; it's important to me to be wild in the way I define it like I don't walk anybody's path.

When asked about defining wild, Maya shifts ever so slightly in her seat, adjusts her glasses, and stares at me. I feel the intensity of the gaze through the fiberoptics connecting us. I find myself shifting in my seat. Not because I'm uncomfortable by the intensity of the gaze. But because the gaze is not condemning, in the way that Black women often experience the gaze, the white male gaze for example, but because it is inviting. This is part of our "songversation," capturing the dialectic nature of testifying.

"I don't walk anybody's path," *Maya says.*

As I watch Badu's "Window Seat" video at the end when she is "assassinated" and speaks of playing it safe, not walking in truth but following the groupthink, I hear Maya's words, "I don't walk anybody's path" *somewhat differently. I don't hear it as a place of defiance but a place of deeply knowing self and claiming the space she needed to be in her truth. And I find myself wondering whether Maya has been fined for walking her truth. How was she fined when she discarded the clothing (metaphorically) that we are expected to wear, laying bare in front of society?*

Well, I would say it's important to be yourself and even if you say your authentic self, you're . . . you are drawn to say the words with something . . . someone says authentic. I mean, that's . . . that's out here. I say be wild. Be! Allow yourself to like what you like, to love what you love. Like, being wild to me is reading poetry. You know, and like really, really enjoying it. And I, I wasn't taught to read poetry. It wasn't something that I knew Black women did.

???. Question marks are what I wrote in the margins as I read this. I was unsure what Maya was trying to articulate at the beginning of her response. And I thought of not including it. However, I opted to include it here as I think it is important for showing how we testify and as a way of staying true to what I state in chapter 1 that I will privilege the voices of the women who inform Erotic Testimonies and that I would not change their testimony. As I sat more with this part of Maya's testimony, I was able to see how her words show how we work through our testimony and how it becomes clearer the more we engage with it. And so, I allowed Maya's

words to just be. Being wild is about allowing yourself to be and not having it defined by others.

I find myself moaning, the way the women moaned when another was in the act of testifying. Drawn into the person's words, their essence. "To love what you love." I scribbled in the margins. When was the last time you checked in about are you doing what you love? And I also think of "Poetry Is Not a Luxury" and how Lorde speaks to engaging the self. In "Poetry Is Not a Luxury" Lorde (1984) writes,

> The quality of light by which we scrutinize our lives has direct bearing upon the product which we live, and upon the changes which we hope to bring about through those lives. It is within this light that we form those ideas by which we pursue our magic and make it realized. (36)

How do Black women not just pursue the magic but also make it real? In Black Girl Magic Beyond the Hashtag, *we argue that a tremendous amount of work goes into making magic. As we suggest, Black-identified girls and women are engaged in a* "radical democratic practice by claiming space for their actuations of self" *(Jordan-Zachery and Harris 2019, 21) by engaging in labor and sometimes hard labor. Poetry, in part, allows Maya the space she needs to do the work of making magic. Poetry provides Maya with the space to enter the interior, the* "Dream Space" *(see Alexander 2004, 5), where she is able to cultivate her Black feminine self outside of the narratives of race and gender, for example, while still recognizing the functioning of race-gender oppression. And as she suggests, she works to claim this space.*

The sweetness of Maya's words draws me in. I asked her to tell me how others responded/respond to her wildness. And how is that response based on her being simultaneously Black and woman.

Well, you know, when I was a child, I really didn't understand race. I didn't see the difference. . . . And it really wasn't until even in junior high school. I didn't really understand, or I didn't [*trails off*]. I wasn't troubled by racism because it didn't bother me; nothing bothered me. I enjoyed everything except math, I was terrible, but I really enjoyed walking to school and friends. It was when President Kennedy got killed, I was fourteen, and suddenly I realized there was, there was, this real thing happening, and I think in my growing up, we were very religious, Jewish—Black, Jewish people. And so, there wasn't a lot of political information floating, we went to temple, that was our focus. But when I got into high school, when I got into college, that's when I began to understand in a deeper sense, that I wasn't supposed to be this free person, that there were, there were things that I should be aware of, like I should be a certain way. It was important to me to be me in my private time, but not just the wild me that I had been accustomed to. So, I really love to read books. So reading was part of my being wild, and it wasn't what everybody did. Yeah. Like, I, I wouldn't, I wouldn't, talk about my love of books. I wouldn't talk about . . . I guess that was the most profound thing in my life, you know, really just books and understanding, and words . . . meant a lot to me. When I realized about racism, it sort of put a cloak around me in terms of being in public because I realized [*that*] I was being treated differently.

I find myself lingering on Maya's use of the term "private time"—why is this part of her testimony resonating with my spirit? I circled this, went back, and underlined it. Private time. I suspect that private time is simply more than those moments when we get away from others, even our loved ones and that private time can even happen in public. I am imagining that private time is that moment when we are able to get into our interior. Those moments when we are not laboring for others. In that quiet time, in the words of Badu, we get "A look around," *the opportunity to determine what it is we need as she sings about, the opportunity to confront the duality so many of us face. We get to see ourselves, to come back in. Thus, Maya's poetry reading coupled with her understanding of private time can be read as a means by which she goes into the interior to find and experience her wildness.*

It was only after I had meditated and came to Badu's song that I consciously realized that Maya spoke of her racial recognition in relation to Kennedy's assassination. Audre truly knew what she was speaking of when she told me to let the ancestors guide because this was not a conscious decision to use Badu's song alongside Maya's experience. I wish I could claim that I intentionally did this, but that would be a lie.

Beyond this, I think: What does it mean when Black women insert themselves into white male spaces/narratives? Badu and Maya insert Black female bodies into a space, literal and imagined, that was constructed as white and male—the space of President Kennedy's assassination. The use of this space speaks to self-realization and self-actualization. It speaks to how Black women work to address the politics of invisibility that they often experience. They claim a window seat to both see and be seen according to their desires.

Well, the first thing is I knew I was different. So, I think being different gave me the permission to be myself. What's very interesting is when you think of wild, you think of somebody who's wild and all over the place. I was a quiet person. Do you know what I mean? Like, I'm sure I had in my adult time, there were times when I loved to party and do things. But I had children, and I had my first child at sixteen. And so that did put a damper over me because I was a mother—that sort of changed things. But I think being in a different religion that no one was in as a Black person enabled me to be myself, and, and . . . to be myself and be wild, and that is not wild as defined by our culture. I'm talking wild as defined by Audre Lorde.

It's so narrow. I mean, like the way I cook, the way I decide meals, the way I try to just be free and wild and it's with my food, it's, it's definitely with music. I'll listen to whatever I want. I don't care that I'm a Black woman. I do care. But you know what I mean.

No, I'm very lucky that . . . I haven't felt limited by being myself, like I always felt I had the privilege of being. It was a privilege to be a human being, and it was a privilege for me to be me. And I think early on, like, I started reading and studying spiritual works. So, in spiritual poetry and the Bible and when you read some of those Bible stories, they are wild, so I could vision myself back in being the woman in Sodom and Gomorrah who looked back, you know? And the dancing during that time. I just think I may be a hard case because I was steeped in reading and music.

The presence of Yemayá is in Maya's chuckle. The way she sometimes ends her sentences with a chuckle, a sense of satisfaction seems to permeate the air. It invites in quiet and reflection. I think of all the times music and the words of Black women have afforded me that space I needed just to be me, to invite in quiet and reflection, how they have afforded me the opportunity to come to know me deeper.

I can't remember my first incidence of racism. One that's profound to me is that I was in college, and I wrote a story about a man who was a murderer, a killer. I probably called him a murderer, a serial killer we would have called him. And there were two Black people in this class and everybody, they were so angry with me for, like writing about how we can be [*trails off*] that we have the depth and breadth to be everything and [*trails off*]. I remember [*trails off*] they were really pissed at me that I made the killer a Black man and not . . . Just why did I have to say he was Black? Why couldn't he just be Joe Jones or whoever it was? And it seemed important to me that we be able to have every everything that everyone else could have, whether it was something negative or positive, bad, or good. You know, I felt we were supposed to be like, good and . . . you learn, you've got to keep yourself neat and clean, and you look a certain way and you speak a certain way, and it's all being in communication with "the white man."

"Communication with 'the white man.' *" I scribbled the word lines in the margin of my notes as I listened to Maya tell how she's been trained to center white maleness—the ideology. Lines: as Black girls, we are taught to walk and navigate racial and gender lines. Tiptoeing around the scripts and stereotypes (Jordan-Zachery 2017) that center whiteness. Protective lines are designed to save us from harm but cause harm in their way. Robbing us of our sense of being while offering us a way of being. Dichotomies of being a Black girl/woman. Disembodiment. We experience disembodiment which, according to Sekile Nzinga-Johnson (2013, 11),* "lead[s] many to exist and persist disjointedly as intellectual workers." *I wonder what our lives would be like if we didn't have these lines. I wonder what our work would be like and if we are able to rise up from it feeling* "empowered" *(Lorde 1984, 55).*

Those Deep Places: The Interior

Now for interior.

Rich.

This word hangs as I ask Maya to tell me what she thinks about when she hears the word interior. Like a stalactite, "rich" is there simple and majestic yet dripping with so much more.

You know, there are so many things that you can experience in life like my son died from [*trails off*]. So that was death and [*trails off*].

A quiet moment presents itself. I let it be what it needs to be.

Other losses, and I feel like I have a deep interior because I can live with those and get something from understanding death. Although I don't know what's beyond any more than anyone else, but I understand how life, you know, I understand principles of life that everything changes and the process that we have is we live, and we die. So, I understand that, and I accept that. So, my interior gets . . . gets supported by everything that happens, and it gets enriched, by, by, the words, by the challenges some people have [*trails off*]. There's a thing like I, long ago, stopped having judgment about others. And I think that gave me a rich interior, my acceptance of people. Now, that acceptance doesn't mean I'm going to let you do anything negative to me or walk over me or treat me in a way that I don't want, is not respectful. No, but it's like being able to see and accept, you know, this person has to do this, whether it's drinking or dancing or being loud or doing things that may not be what I do, but I can. I used to when I was younger, I would like pooh-pooh and shake my head. I don't do it, and I don't know if that's age, but I think, in my middle age, middle years, I was more judgmental. But I think by freeing myself, the inner landscape of me gets fuller and richer. And that's not to any point. That's not to achieve anything. You've got to know that just being self is not to, to, be like anyone, to achieve anything, to go high, to go low. It's like just being, just being.

But in a way, my interior is like a combination of tapestries. And then this tapestry can have something that massages my concerns about the world. And then it'd be like a great soup that makes, brings me comfort. It can make me very annoyed and angry, you know, or I can get . . . I can I always want to talk about literature. I can get the rise from James Baldwin. Right now, I'm reading Ta-Nehisi Coates. He just did what you call that, edited one of those magazines, *Vanity Fair*. Wonderful pieces in it.

Maya articulates the notion of our interior being a tapestry that is informed by our experiences, that allows us to determine how we want to enter and be with those outside of ourselves—how we want to feel. Getting to know the interior is less about a means to an end but about being able to sit with oneself so that you can sit in the company of others. Lorde (1984) writes,

> The erotic functions for me in several ways, and the first is in providing the power which comes from sharing deeply any pursuit with another person. The sharing of joy, whether physical, emotional, psychic, or intellectual, forms a bridge between the sharers which can be the basis for understanding much of what is not shared between them, and lessens the threat of their difference. (56*)*

As I listen to Maya, I engage this notion of the erotic that allows us to be with others without demanding that they conform to our lines. Living the erotic allows for our differences to be less threatening as this happens; we are able to go deeper into our interior, the rich and lush place. Thus, we are able to transcend the suspicions and competition often required by racialized heteronormative capitalism.

Layers. As she speaks about going deeper into the interior I imagine Yemayá's seven-layer skirt. And I think of how Badu shed her layers so that she could get beyond walking in the shadows ofothers. Cloaked and naked existing simultaneously. Yemayá and Badu, both freeing in their own way. Not forced to live in a dichotomy, having to make a choice that may not be in one's best interest. Both. Simultaneously. Cloaked and naked. I see Black wild women claiming what they need to be who they were sent to be. I see "Evolved."

The Cosmos: Spirituality Is Connecting Me to Everything

Now, spirituality. What comes to mind?

Expansive, this was scribbled next to the word spirituality. We were now almost thirty minutes into the "songversation," and I had to remind myself to keep posing the words. I found myself wanting to dwell a bit more on how Maya understood wild. I was glad that I allowed us to move on with the "songversation" and that I was able to dwell in this verse of Maya's testimony.

Spirituality for me is that . . . making or having a connection . . . beyond myself, beyond this particular landscape of the world. But it's connected to something that's, I don't want to say greater, but *[trails off]*. That's . . . the world, that's larger than the world. It's like when I think of spirituality, I think of the *Bhagavad Gita* and there was an incarnation of Krishna who was the charioteer for Arjuna, and he's trying to show him how what it is, what everything is.[2] And he stretches his arms out, and within all of his being and his body is the cosmos.

And I see spirituality as my connection to all of that, you know, so it includes God. It includes God, as we know. And I was raised Jewish, but I know God is God in the, in the way you'd look it up in a book. So, it's everything. Spirituality is connecting to everything. And those that are . . . that I can see and touch and then those that are beyond my understanding. I understand about all of the world [trails off], all of life that occurred previous to this moment and that's spirituality.

As I listen to Maya speak of spirituality, I thought of the work of Donna Aza Weir-Soley (2009, 7) and her claim that "spirituality [is] central to black female subject formation." *It is part of what we use to make ourselves into our image—the magic that some reference when they speak of "Black Girl Magic." Coming back to "Uses of the Erotic," Lorde reminds us that the source of knowledge and power, the erotic, is accessed, in part, through the spiritual realm. Lorde understands spiritual as both* "psychic and emotional" *(1984, 56). According to Lyndon Gill (2018, 8), spirituality is one element of the erotic that* "represent[s] a negotiation of the tension between and ideal vision and our lived reality." *Lorde posits that the erotic is a bridge, a bridge between the spiritual and the political. Spirituality, in conjunction with our political and sensual desires, once recognized and tapped into, allows for change, individual and collective, according to Lorde.*

One Finger Connected to the Divine

When asked about divine, Maya responds,

First thing is elder. I think there is something that happens when people reach a certain stage, and I'm talking about elders and I'm thinking of elders from our elders like, you know, our meaning Black people's elders who hold, within them, the stories, the recipes to the [*trails off]* Life, they hold life

No, ask it again because I just lost . . .

When someone becomes an elder, they have like one finger connected to the divine. So, they're going on and they could live to be one hundred. So, I can't quantify how old the elder is because you could also see that in a younger person. But for me, it starts with the elder, it's the storyteller, the . . . it's the grandmothers and the great, great, great-grandmothers. And it's what they gave to us or left with us, it becomes divine. The artifacts, the histories, all of that divine, and then, there are people who manifest the divine in their being.

Well, you know, there are people who have like divine/ sacred, seems divine, seems very closely aligned to sacred.

Ah, we're gonna get there. So, tell me about sacred, go ahead.

Oh, OK. But I see the two almost being synonymous and . . . So, it doesn't [*trails off*]. I can't fit it into one category. I mean, one type of individual, because sacred can be anything, you know, anything that you revere, not in a worldly sense, but in another or otherworldly or godly sense could become sacred. It can be, it can be a pen that you revere. And this becomes sacred because it means something to you

Holding my favorite pen. When I say I love all pens, but this one is very pretty.

She laughs as if she's seen the funniest thing ever. I think it is important to recognize how Maya laughs as it is part of her testimony. I see her laughter as part of a metasystem, part of the sensual/sensuality that Lorde references, that bends time and space. Allowing access for us to see and to see beyond what is presented to us in the here and now.

So divine to me means . . . [What] first comes to mind is elder, sacred is whatever you have that means something great to you or means something. And you feel moved by listening to it, singing to it, eating it, seeing it, speaking about it. Sometimes you'll hear people; they're talking in a regular tone and suddenly they'll say Dr. Martin Luther King [*speaks in a lower, softer tone*] used to feel that they revere this, you know what I mean? So, they may not even be aware of it, but they are seeing him as sacred. So, their visage changes, and their voice will change. You've seen that with people hunkered down and they're like, sister Bell? You know, it's true, isn't it?

It happens because sacred and divine are words that are beyond—they're metaphysical words, even though [they] are in the dictionary. It's beyond, it's beyond the realm of what we understand.

Holders of life—the elders and the ancestors. Sacred knowledge. I scribble in the margins. This brings me to Alice Walker.

> What I'm doing is literarily trying to reconnect us to our ancestors. All of us. I'm really trying to do that because I see that ancient past as the future, that the connection that was original is a connection: if we can affirm it in the present, it will make a different future. Because it's really fatal to see yourself as separate. (Walker 1989, 31)

Walker and Maya speak to the link between the past, present, and future—a continuity of time—and as defined by the ancestors. And I find myself thinking of what continuity of time means for Black women, especially in the context of the institution of slavery, colonialism, and neocolonialism that gives way to violence and the ripping of our family members away from us. How do we mark time and how is time valuable for not seeing oneself as separate? Walker says that we make a new future and that we do this through recollection. And that's maybe how as Black women we mark time, we engage in the recollection of stories (including myths) left for us by our elders and our ancestors. We do this so that we can be whole, whole even in the context of oppressive structures.

It's All to My Eye Feminine

When I think of being feminine, I think of, of, of everything I love, you know, I love feminine. I learned feminine from the world, feminine was taught to me.

Well, through magazines, through books, through descriptions in books, through stories. It just, it tells you what feminine means, you know, and it's, it's, not womanly, but feminine embraces certain things like softness, like certain colors. I see a very corally, pinkish, not red, but, but, not pink either. I see like azure blue as feminine. I, see, yeah those are about it. I like that orangey. And then the blue-green color.

It's fascinating to me that Maya didn't pick colors that are in a standard color palette. Like your basic red or blue. She picked colors that sit somewhere between the reds and the pinks and the blues and the greens. And they flow depending on how you look at it. I'm reminded of the Caribbean Sea and how different parts can hold different shades and how as a little girl I would delight in watching the various shades of "blue." And so, depth, vastness, and mystery come to mind as I think of how Maya speaks of her love of colors. Complexity and depth—like Yemayá, her seven-layered skirt that flows in a sensual way as she emerges from the ocean. The seven layers holding space, the type of space that is needed to help others heal. The seven layers holding stories we need to recollect to be whole—stories of abuse, care, vengeance, and healing. Stories of self-valuation and self-definition. Swirling in the in-between, that place where feelings rest, like the colors Maya describes.

I'm also fascinated by Maya's suggestion that feminine is not womanly. I wonder what if anything is wrong with being womanly. Why draw this line? I question my thought that there is a line being drawn. There is so much to think about. I think of how as a society we make distinctions between the slut and the virgin. I often ask my students to define what constitutes promiscuous as it relates to a woman. I ask how many partners must a woman have to be considered promiscuous? They often cannot answer. Yet we use these lines to make distinctions, to categorize, to reward and to punish.

I searched to see if I could uncover a Black feminist understanding of womanly and feminine. There was something about the distinction that Maya was making that was intriguing to me. Celeste Henery (a dear friend and research associate of African and African Diaspora Studies at the University of Texas Austin), via an email exchange (December 21, 2020) helped me to explore what I may have been sensing when Maya made a distinction between womanly and feminine. Celeste wrote:

> Part of the impulse towards the feminine rather than womanly might be a desire to moveaway from particular women's identities, for example, motherhood as the most loaded one, particularly for black women. My reading is that black motherhood has been historically demeaned yet gained a legible status. It is recognized, but limiting for black women . . . as it is not sexualized, and thus constructed as not feminine . . . e.g., mammy.
>
> Furthermore, it is an all defining identity (motherhood) that limits black women, in particular, from being seen in other ways. The impulse towards the feminine conjures something apart from children and women's labors.

Maybe Maya is working within the discursive constructions that tend to limit Black women, those constructions that tell them to sit their wild behinds down for example. Thus, to move beyond these limiting discursive constructions, Maya conjures softness. A type of softness that is not always available to the idea of being womanly in a racialized context.

I find myself lingering on the notion of softness.

Softness is not always an aesthetic or narrative afforded to Black women. As I think of the scripts and stereotypes often ascribed to Black women, I am reminded of how softness, and feminine by default, tend not to be included. Stereotypes such as the strong Black woman, Sapphire, welfare queen, or even the ass script I write about in Shadow Bodies, suggest a hardness (what might be associated with masculine energy). The institution of slavery often categorized Black women as less feminine in comparison to white women (see Washington 1990). As a result, Black women have to imagine and create themselves as soft (and soft should not be read as passivity for example).

This brings me back to Erykah Badu. Badu sings "Concluding/Concentrating on my music, lover, and my babies/Makes me wanna ask the lady for a ticket outta town/So can I get a window seat . . . /So, in my mind I'm tusslin'/Back and forth 'tween here and hustlin' " *How is this a pull between womanly and feminine? A cry for softness is to return to that* "feminine plane" *that Audre Lorde speaks to. It's the ability to feel, and deeply, to live fully across a wide spectrum as Badu seems to long for. It is the tension that she sings about—living only on one plane while longing for a fuller and richer experience. It is that tension that Lorde (1984) writes about,*

> As women, we have come to distrust that power which rises from our deepest and non-rational knowledge. We have been warned against it all our lives by the male world, which values this depth of feeling enough to keep women around in order to exercise it in the service of men, but which fears this same depth too much to examine the possibilities of it within themselves. So women are maintained at a distant/inferior position to be psychically milked, much the same way ants maintain colonies of aphids to provide a lifegiving substance for their masters. (53–54)

And so, when Black women choose to feel, expansively, and to live their truths and deeply; but, it goes against how society tends to conceptualize the erotic. When the erotic is kept only on one plane it does not allow us to live fully and with joy across all the work that we do. It does not allow us to be wild, wild Black women.

But I'm left to wonder, what does imagining ourselves as soft then allow us to do?

What feminine means to me, is let's see. I don't know. I like *[trails off]*. I know I'm feminine.

I ask: How do you know that you are feminine?

Only from what I've learned. From the external. But I know that being myself, like, I love flowers. I like fragrance.

Let's talk about fragrance. So, when you think feminine and you think, Maya, and you think fragrance what are you smelling?

I'm smelling rose, and lavender, and jasmine.

How are these scents used in herbal medicine? That is what I scribbled in the margin. In aromatherapy and herbal medicine rose oil is said to ease pain and depressive symptoms. Lavender is said to also ease pain and is sometimes used to lessen headaches and anxiety, for example. And jasmine is used as an aphrodisiac, antiseptic, and to help with anxiety. I'm finding myself fascinated by the fact that Maya selected scents that are associated with healing and anxiety/depression. And it all makes me think portal and healing. I wonder what this all has to do with being a wild Black woman. In my notes, I underlined my query. Eventually, I begin to understand how and why this is related to the notion of being a wild Black woman.

Vrettos (1989) writes,

> Herbal medicine was commonly practiced by both male and female healers, although Melville J. Herskovits, in his study of Africanisms in diasporic cultures, associates herbal and root medicines with predominantly female modes of healing. While herbal practitioners posed less of a supernatural threat to white authority, both female healers and black healing arts of all varieties were, nevertheless, feared in antebellum America as a challenge to slave control. (460)

As I read Vrettos I scribble "Black women refused to be told to sit down and stop being wild." Indeed, Black women have long been portals of healing that defy Eurocentric understandings of how to heal. They tapped into a reservoir of healing traditions designed to bring together the mind and body. Maya seems to have tapped into this history of healing and her naming of these scents hints at such; we also see this in her work with yoga. Her biography on the Kripalu Center for Yoga and Health's website reads in part, "Her teaching combines traditional forms with her own indigenous wisdoms, encouraging individuals to use yoga to renew their spirit, change their consciousness, and embrace healthy living."

In her 2010 interview with Lebovits, Maya explained how she came to the practice of yoga. She said,

> It was a difficult time: I had three teenaged children, was beginning a recovery program for alcohol abuse, and healing from cancer surgery. In addition, I was caring for a brother battling AIDS. After years of practicing, my true life began to unfold. The practice of yoga did for me what no substance, doctor, support group, family member, friend, or lifestyle change could do. Yoga introduced me to my inner self.

Yoga was/is Maya's vessel for healing. Through the practice of yoga, she is able to enter the interior and come out into a place of wholeness, which is truth. So her chosen scents make perfect sense.

I think when I was younger, like I didn't need the feminine when I was a young woman. I was just beautiful and wild, and I never thought about it. You know, I was just a woman, . . . I still don't study it or work on it, but I think, like, I like pretty things, not too, not wishy-washy, I don't like that, but I like beauty, but it's all to my eye, you know what I mean?

And the notion that sometimes you simply know. There are ways of knowing that wild Black women seem to tap into. Some may call it intuition, for example. But it is a way of knowing that transcends time and space, as it is a part of our spiritual and even cultural ways of knowing, where the erotic serves as the bridge. To some, it may seem nonrational, but Lorde (1984, 35) warns us about discounting or not trusting our ways of knowing—our feelings. Distrusting our ways of knowing takes us outside of our interior and consequently our ability to tap into our power. When our access to our erotic is limited, we cannot name ourselves and our desires. Maya offers us a glimpse into the value of using the erotic and how she practices such use to engage in self-articulation

There Is Energy in Stillness

Now for the word energy.

Well, movement comes to mind first. And as an elder, now, my energy is very different. Becoming this age, I don't have lots of energy. I don't have that physical energy. Beyond physical energy. Oh! Beyond physical energy. Well, there's the energy of thought, you know, there is an energy in thought. There is an energy in resting in just doing nothing. There's energy in stillness. I do a particular meditation, or there are times when I just practice stillness, meaning I'm going to be still for ten, fifteen minutes.

But that seems to go against what capitalism tells us, right?

I know.

I think so. I won't go there. I refuse to be *[trails off]* I won't live my life by somebody else's concepts or ideas. I mean, there are certain things that we must do. You must pay your taxes. You must pay your bills. You must get sleep and eat. But other than that, those things that I have to do, I want to be totally free.

Maya speaks about what bell hooks (1995) named white supremacist capitalist patriarchy imperialism. It is a way of thinking of how Black individuals, particularly women, in this case, engage in and with the very tensions and oppressions we face. This has given way to women like Maya unmaking what it means to be Black and woman in relation to these systems of oppression. In Maya, I see Harriet Jacobs and her desire to be free and the long history of Black women who sought to unmake what it means to be Black and woman—the narratives that are often imposed from outside.

Jacobs tells of her experiences of sexual violence at the hands of her owner and chronicles her journey to freedom. In her quest for freedom, Jacobs went into the interior; she hid in a storeroom crawlspace from 1835 until 1842. As Miranda Green-Barteet (2013, 54) writes, "Jacobs is, however, more in control of her body and her life while in the garret than she has been at any other time of her life. Jacobs identifies the garret as an empowering location and uses the power of its interstitiality to her advantage." *In the garret, Jacobs went into the physical interior, thereby tapping into her interior, that place where the political, spiritual, and sensual meet, in her quest for freedom.*

I imagine that when Maya says that she wants to be free, she is speaking to the same space that Jacobs tapped into, and this is why she has worked for herself for several years—as a way of having control over her being. Lorde (1984) tells us that,

> The principal horror of any system which defines the good in terms of profit rather than in terms of human need, or which defines human need to the exclusion of the psychic and emotional components of that need—the principal horror of such a system is that it robs our work of its erotic value. (55)

Jacobs's body was put to work as she was an enslaved individual, and she was forced to engage in sexual activity; her offspring, and thus her reproductive "labor," was stripped from her. Slavery sought to rob Jacobs of her erotic. But she fought to make herself into whom she knew she was to be free—by going into the interior, both in terms of physical space and in terms of that political, spiritual, and sensual space that Lorde describes. Maya is part of that long legacy of wild Black women. Like Maya's grandmother, Jacobs is part of the divine, the cosmos, that energy that Maya describes. And she can tap into this divine feminine power to resist those structures that seek to take her away from her erotic.

The Music and the Spirit Bring Joy

Now let's talk about joy.

Well, I know that joy can be deep, but there's like surface joy, like just a great big ole smile, a great big ole laugh, or something silly. That's joy. And I think joy takes many different forms *[pause]*. It comes in many different forms and has different perspectives. I spoke to my twelve-year-old grandson today, and it was such joy just to hear him say, "Hey, Nanny." I felt such joy when he says, "Hey, Nanny." All nasally, you know?

I just think joy has to be subjective and . . . it just, I don't know, I like to feel joyful—the most joy, like when I go to [*trails off*]. I'm Jewish, but we have a Black church, and we express joy through singing, and prancing, and movement. So that's the most innocent, I'd say, joy, other than the birth of my grandson or something. But going to a service and having the music and the spirit bring you joy. There's no reason, but you're feeling like, wow, this is great. I'm feeling happy, or joyful because I'm praising God, you know. Joy to me comes in many, many forms, but the most profound experience I've had was just praising God where I was like, this is joy, right!

I scribbled in the margins, "found God in me, and loved her fiercely" *(Ntozake Shange). And I wonder about the relationship between singing and dancing and praising God and feeling joyful. I would often watch women become trance-like in their praise and worship during service. Some would laugh, shout, cry, or sit and rock back and forth. Some would dance. Was it joy? Did it allow them a form of release or transcendence if it was joy? An opportunity to leave the earthly sorrows behind? I think of my gran and how I would watch her give praise, sometimes getting into the spirit. It would seem like she had left her body and/or this dimension. My young mind could not fully comprehend but could sense that these women and my gran were tapping into something beyond the physical or material realm—a sacred space, the erotic. In speaking of her worship experiences, Maya embodies this sense of the erotic—the bringing together of the body and the spirit. She enters a sacred space. And I wonder, do my gran and Maya meet God in themselves?*

Erotic: Positive Expression for Oneself

The erotic, what do you imagine or think of?

That's the first thing I think of erotic. Erotic means sexual . . . it describes sex in some kind of way. But I do think erotic is—can be deeper than that and fuller than that, you know. I think erotic has one meaning when you're younger and another meaning when you're older.

Maya thinks of time and the passage of time and how our understandings evolve, giving way to new and different meanings as we grow older. I also noticed this when she spoke of the divine, for example.

Let's see erotic is, it's not a pleasant-sounding word.

Again, there is laughter. But this time, it seems to signal something different than when she spoke of her pen. When she spoke of the pen, the laughter hand an airy quality; this laughter seems deeper, but it is not sinister. She leans back into her seat and closes her eyes ever so briefly after she's done laughing. I wonder what crossed her mind in that brief moment. I wonder if erotic has a less than pleasant sound because it may be connected to sex. And sex can, at times, be a taboo subject. She is my elder, so I find myself timid to ask the questions that enter my mind. In this moment, I recognize that I'm within the lines. I'm coloring within the lines.

I love words; it's not [*trails off*]. But you know, you can take things like the [*trails off*], you can make things if it's important to you, you can give it that sexual slant, or you can give it a more holistic perspective. Where facets of erotic may help, may be important to you in different areas of your life. I don't know what areas because I do align it with physical sex. But I think as you grow and you learn, you can have a product by definition, erotic moments without sex. You can be erotic through listening to music, looking at art, dancing, and drumming. And good conversation can be erotic without it being an erotic conversation. So that's looking at erotic as a positive expression for oneself. And then you risk when you make it a positive expression for oneself; you risk that others aren't going to understand how you're interpreting it.

Risk of coloring outside of the lines/margins and it not being recognized but treated as something bad or wrong, so we find ourselves self-policing. Yet Maya suggests a form of meaning-making that allows her to redefine these lines.

Well, I like to think I made tacos the other night, and to me, it was such an erotic meal. Mm-hmm. And I think it was. I don't make tacos often, but it was just the [*trails off*]. It was, it was interesting. All the various textures, the ground meat, the sautéed stuff, I even put cabbage, which I thought really made it a rather erotic, red cabbage. So, I think food can be erotic, but it always moves us to that close to sex kind of thing. And I'm saying it can be more than that. Yes, but I don't know what it is, but it's more than that because I remember I was like, really? I was excited to make these tacos.

We talk about food and food preparation and how it allows for wildness. Food preparation allows Maya to experience sensuality—touch, and smell. Through her detailing of the experience of preparing tacos, Maya shows how she experiences engaging the self, thereby tapping into her inte-

rior. As I listened to Maya's recount of preparing tacos, I was reminded of the power of the erotic and how it allows us to experience passion when the work we do is aligned with our truth. This allows Maya to move food preparation out of the often patriarchal cast it is often shadowed in. A dominant framework that centers on the heterosexual family (and nation) suggests that women do food preparation as an act of service. Allowing oneself to see this as a sensuous act, something that brings pleasure outside of the performance of meeting another's needs provides the space for the countering of dissemblance that may arise from a heteronormative understanding of food preparation.

According to Baker-Fletcher (2004, 202), in her description of Eros, Sexuality, and Black Folk, *she describes this mix as,* "A love of good music, food, roundness, and good lovemaking that satisfies the soul as well as the body." *Further, she says that the mix of eros, sexuality, and Blackness* "go together in traditional Black folk culture like smoked meat in greens. It forms a rich cultural code that works toward abundant life." *I suspect that is why Maya felt that taco making was erotic; because in its sensuality, it offered a sense of abundance that transcends the material world.*

Again, I noticed that I wrote the word expansive in the margin. And I wonder why I seem to come back to this word. Maybe as I listen to Maya describe her making of tacos and her way of worship, I imagine an expansive space that is deeply satisfying to the mind, body, and soul. I looked at my notes and scribbled beneath expansive: richness, abundance, deep. Worship and food preparation all seem to hold these qualities for Maya.

What else is erotic is good sheets on your bed.

100 [*thread*] or more cotton sheets are terrific, girl.

Just so for me, it's like my art, like, I do this thing with my left hand, I'm right-handed, and I make art with my left hand. And it's, it's, just very . . . if you want to use erotic, it's erotic.

Oh, that's OK, and prayer. Don't forget prayer; prayer can be [*trails off*].

Oh, prayer is one of the things that I quite enjoy doing. When I was in India, I studied how to pray with a group of priests, and I really have a lot of joy, praying in the different ways that I've learned, you know? I know that I'm connecting with I want to say the divine, the all cosmological being or entity because I have no idea really what it is.

But I love prayer because one should pray; one might pray to God as a brother, as a sister, as a cousin, as a friend, as a parent. And when you pray, and you put on that garment of, I am praying to my brother, it's just wonderful! I learned that the vessel is to humanize, to put your prayer in, give it a quality to it. And let me tell you this. I'm the first one to say, Lord, help me right from my lips.

And, you know, it's like when there's . . . when something's happening, I forget all the methodologies. I'm like, Lord, help me with that basic. You can just ask, and it's it really works for me.

When my son Marko passed away, I remember saying, Lord help me. And that was the only thing that would give me some kind of calm, you know. I would say, Lord, help me and just sit. Or I'd be in my car; I'd have to pull off the road. Lord, help me. It just was what it was all I could say, it was all I could say. And I don't know how or why, but I was helped to do it.

According to Lorde (1982, 91), "Our feelings are our most genuine paths to knowledge." *And we see this with how Maya uses prayer. Prayer—the sacred and the erotic seem to come together for Maya when she prays. While she speaks of her religion as a Black Jew, I get the sense that prayer becomes more than just a religious practice. For her, praying seems to take on erotic energy, capturing how Lorde speaks of the erotic as spiritual life energy. In essence, Maya is cultivating subjectivity by allowing herself to engage her feelings and to engage them in an expansive way across multiple domains. This is not a practice that is always encouraged, as society tends to privilege productivity and rational thought over sensuality; therefore, telling us that the mind should dominate the body. Maya works outside of this narrative—listening to the knowledge of her feelings, accessed through the stillness that takes her into her erotic. And this is what makes Maya a wild Black woman.*

Chapter 4

It's Just Easier to Fuck

Sekile's Testimony

Prelude IV

How I was first introduced to Sekile is a bit of a mystery to me. What I know is that I have known Sekile for a while now. Long enough to witness our children go off to college, moving from childhood through teen years to young adulthood. And we navigated academia together, moving, settling in, and moving again, often lamenting about how academia mistreats Black women and those at the margins. Through the years, we discussed our writing projects, moaning, laughing, and feeling exhilarated by it all and sometimes all simultaneously. And in the midst of it all, we have shared a journey of growing deeper into our Black feminine selves. And what a journey it has been!

~

It's 3 p.m. EST, and we connect by Zoom. Sekile is sitting in front of a window that is undressed; no blinds, no curtains; it seems to suggest an openness, all the while intoning that it is talking back to me—daring me to enter in. With her beautiful grey tresses combed to one side, the other side is short but not buzz-cut; Sekile greets me, "Hey, sis." Gum popping, earring dangling, she sits in her full elegance. I smile as the image of that New York 1980s B-girl pops into my head, and this is only reinforced as

I think of "Push It" by Salt-N-Pepa. In talking about what it means to be a B-girl, B-girl Chyna says,

> Battles give women an opportunity to show a side of them that's not necessarily socially acceptable. You go to a battle and the idea is to be aggressive, really offensive, like you're attacking somebody. That's not something you can do in your normal day life; you're expected to be polite and ladylike. Breaking is an opportunity to talk shit, be angry, and be a badass, and it's cool. You suck if you can't do that. (Cooper and Kramer 2005, 57)

B-girl Chyna is speaking of break dancing, but there is so much more that she is invoking. As I read her words, I'm reminded of how women, Black women on the margins specifically, engage their race and gender, thus taking control of their subjectivity.

CONTROL

The type of control that Janet Jackson sang about. The kind of control that I imagined as I listened to her album on repeat (see chapter 1).

Sekile, like B-girl Chyna, is engaged in controlling her subjectivity, and this is why I think of bell hooks as I write up her testimony. bell hooks (1989a, 14), feminist scholar and activist, states that the "power of voice as gesture of rebellion and resistance" is substantively different from regular or ordinary talk. And this is no regular talk that Sekile is engaging us in. Sekile's voice is beautifully modulated, serene in its tone, yet it belies an intensity that one feels compelled to lean into. She takes us through this polemical and purposeful expedition of how she navigates both the personal and professional. As a result, we have this beautifully woven tapestry of how she calls on the erotic.

An erotic that speaks to:

> self-identification,
> self-representation, and
> self-realization

hooks takes us on this journey of understanding how Black women talk back to oppression in hopes of making themselves real—and real in a substantive manner. And this is how I interact with Sekile's testimony. This is a testimony of self—identification, representation, and realization. My engagement with Sekile's testimony is shaped, in part, by Black feminist theorists and critic bell hooks, the color red (and not some bright red, but this intense red color that seems to have traces of black and other colors mixed in), the African goddess Ashiakle, and crescent moons. The soundtrack that plays in my mind is "Push It" by Salt-N-Pepa.

The moon,
often thought of as a goddess,
is envisaged as a female entity
Representing rhythm, cycles, and fertility

The crescent moon
Brings us to
growth, creativity, and manifestation

Ashiakle is thought of as the goddess of wealth. She is worshiped throughout Ghana and is considered the ruler of the sea and its treasures. Associated with Ashiakle are the colors red and white.

Red embodies	**White symbolizes**
Death	Death
Destruction	Beauty
Heat	Creation
Power	Spirituality
	Water
	Wealth
	Femininity

But I recognize that the meanings of these colors are not necessarily as neat as they may seem (see Breidenbach 1976). Almost like Sekile, there is complexity. When I think of Sekile's testimony, I see a deep rich red color that, to me, captures her heat and power. This is the type of heat and power that Lorde is calling on us to tap into—a woman's power over her own body, spirit, and sensuality. And this is what allows Sekile to talk back in the manner suggested by hooks. I invite you to be in community with Sekile's testimony.

Wildness Is Freedom and Bearing Witness

When you hear the word wild, what comes to mind? Don't think too hard. Just tell me what pops up.

Freedom. Freedom comes to mind. Wildness has been part of my praxis for; I want to . . . , I guess [*trails off*]. I would say the last five or six years of, like . . . leaning into wildness, and that is a scary and liberating space for me to be. And I say freedom because it's telling me to unbind myself like I think I have spent a lot of my life healing from sexual violence and trying not to get raped again. In doing some of that, I think I'd police my behaviors, from the way I dress to my engagements, even with men, you know, and my sexual desires. All of those things I've repressed because I, I think I was just navigating, like, the trauma of it all.

And so somehow this notion around wildness I've been attracted to as I bear witness to other wild women in history, particularly wild Black women, and so I'm always just tickled by them. Like I'm tickled, particularly when I see them in historic [context][1]. And I'm just like, damn, she was wild in the 1920s?! It just . . . it ends up like gassing me up, and I'm just like, all right! Like I come from a long history of those women! And so, somehow, it emboldens me. And then, all of a sudden, I'm wearing this ridiculously bright-colored vintage clothing that I would not have worn ten years ago. I mean, I really, you know, dressed in grays and browns. And I think part of that was like trying to blend in, trying not to be seen, trying to [*trails off*] as a self-protective mechanism, if you will. And now I'm like, yeah, I'm wearing this ridiculously bright vintage wardrobe that I would not have worn ten years ago! I don't know what was going on in the 50s, 60s, and 70s, but everything was bright and loud. And so, if I'm wearing those clothes, it almost was like [*trails off*] it allowed me to safely take a risk and be wild and free. I think it started with my clothing. I was like, oh, I can wear this thing, and somehow it was connected to my personality. But it was also like forcing me to be seen, if you will, and be comfortable being seen, and that felt freeing.

Black women face many forms of domination based on gender, class, race, or other identity markers, and Sekile names them all within a few minutes of our conversation. In doing so, she reveals her many layers of selfhood. The open window, against which she sits, is but a metaphor of her testimony. Her testimony is viscerally honest and shared most calmly. In my imagination, this mix embodies Lorde's use of the erotic. I say this as I sense that Sekile has come to know herself and know herself deeply. But this practice of knowing self was not always easy, I suspect.

According to the National Organization of Women (n.d.), "For African American women, sexual assault and violence are incredibly pervasive issues that routinely go unreported and under-addressed. Over eighteen percent of African American women will be sexually assaulted in her lifetime." *In the novel* The Color Purple, *Alice Walker takes on the topic of rape and incest. The protagonist, Celie, survives being raped by her stepfather and her husband's abuse. Walker takes us through this daunting tale, and by the end of the novel, we see how Celie is able to do more than just survive.*

Through her interactions with other women, Celie asserts her voice. And this is where I want to rest as I engage with Sekile's testimony. Women's bonding, autonomy, and voice. I do this not to avoid Sekile's truth but to center how she has bonded with women as a way of speaking her truth—another feature of Lorde's uses of the erotic. Sekile sits in community, historical and living (the living is explored below) and finds voice by being in a community of women whom she considers as wild, women who personify the type of freedom she longs for, describes, and lives. She can lean "into wildness" by calling on these women, even if that means bending time by going into the past to be here in the present. Throughout Lorde's body of work, one sees how she uses women's communities/communities of women, real and imagined, to rename and reimagine the world—a more just world. In the epilogue of Zami, *Lorde (1982, 255) writes,* "Recreating in words the women who helped give me substance." *She then goes on to name these women. And this is what Sekile invokes when she says that she is* "leaning into wildness" *through these women that she names, and in so doing, she is able to "be seen, if you will, and be comfortable being seen, you know, and that felt freeing." Lorde and Sekile are creating herstory and telling their truths.*

And then I think after that came behaviors like I started to name my desires and go after things that didn't follow a script. And so, wildness to me is like going off course, like just breaking the rules, going off course, crafting your own narrative, and being disruptive. Yeah, I think I like being disruptive, not just being an ass, but just because people have such assumptions about you. And so, I like to be [*trails off*]. So, being wild is like, you know, reminds me not [to] conform. I don't know if that makes any sense. Like, so having that as an aspiration reminds me to not erase myself, not to go small, not to be compliant, not to be accommodating.

Naming desires
Crafting own narratives
Not to get too small.

Again, this testimony is about naming places of oppressions AND spaces of liberation by talking back. Like Salt-N-Peppa and those B-girls of the 1980s, Sekile offers a narrative that talks back to being forced to draw within the lines. In 1993, Salt-N-Peppa dropped the single "Shoop." They rapped:

The brother had it goin' on with somethin' kinda . . . uh
Wicked, wicked (oooo)—had to kick it
I'm not shy so I asked for the digits
A ho? No, that don't make me

They list their desires and call out a culture that suggests that women do not speak of their sexual desires unless they are willing to be labeled a "ho" (whore/slut). As mentioned in chapter 1, Black women have not been shy about naming their desires.

As Sekile suggests, Black women are not always seen, and this is because of the fear of the uses of the erotic—our abilities to feel, to express what we feel—our truths and to have the expressions of our feelings recognized and not because they are valuable to another or a patriarchal, capitalist, sexist, and racist structure. And so, Black women use the erotic to craft their own narratives, to list their desires, and to do so boldly. And in doing so, they are speaking back to narratives that say: sit your wild behind down, or she too wild for me . . .

Crafting your own narrative and going off script. I think it's almost like it's a charge. I don't know if I'm necessarily always doing it; I think it's one of those things where it reminds me to do it, it's an aspiration, you know.

So, you mentioned that you see these women, Black women in history. Who are some of the women you think about that might be wild for you?

So, Gladys Bentley pops in my head when I said that. Big Mama Thornton. Bessie Smith and Zora Neale Hurston popped in my mind. Eartha Kitt, Grace Jones. But the person I've been drawn to most recently has been Betty Davis, the funkstress. Yeah! So, I don't know if you listen to Betty Davis's music, but she's been resonating with me lately.

And any reason why she just does?

I think it's . . . [*looks away from the camera in thought as she chews her gum*]. I think it's well, for me, again, like coming back to my stuff around fashion. I think I initially fell into her because I found out she was a model, and then I found out she was a singer that was way ahead of her time, and the world just wasn't ready for her. And they defined her as wild. I mean, they wanted her to be like Diana Ross and all these, you know, like these girl groups, and they wanted to contain her. And she refused. She just refused to be contained to this [respectable notion of] a Black woman. Like the way she sang, the way she was, her presence on stage. She just was [*trails off*]. She made people uncomfortable with her sexual freedom and her power. And so, and she was too much. And they always tried to contain her, you know, and she just refused to be contained. And she eventually dropped off into obscurity and just like disappeared because. I think she had a psychic break because they kept wanting her to be disembodied, you know, and so and she just disappeared.

Contained to "this Black woman."

Disembodied. Disappearance.

And then there is the crescent moon—notions of growth, creativity, and manifestation.

From this partial and situated perspective, we see how Sekile works to resist disembodiment and disappearance and at multiple levels. Yet, Sekile shows us how to engage in a project of (re)covery, a project that challenges both disembodiment and disappearance—by speaking. Sekile engages the crescent moon. And this is her wealth (not in a capitalist understanding of wealth), as this is where her power lies. This is probably why I see red, the boldness of her words, and her naming of her experiences, as I allowed the ancestors to guide me through Sekile's testimony as instructed by Audre Lorde.

And, you know, and it's not really clear where she went for many years. But you know what? What we do know is that she might have went to like a mental health facility. So, you know, there was something about her trajectory, and it was stunted because they wanted her to fit in a box, and she was just like this brilliantly wild person. And then also like how Miles Davis, her ex-husband, tried to beat that out of her. So, it wasn't just the music industry; it was her husband. And in a way, she influences his career. And much of what people talk about Miles Davis is his influence after he meets Betty Davis. But nobody fucking talks about that. And then he gets the fucking credit as his career evolves. So, it's just like a fucking classic tale, right? So, she shrinks. She breaks; he blossoms with her influence. But then I think also just the music industry. Right. We see this happen over and over again. Right? So, I think about it when I think about female emcees in hip-hop. Right. It's the same kind of thing. Like I remember, Salt-N-Pepa and people were uncomfortable with their sex-positive lyrics.

But they were being wild and provocative. And I said there was something about that. I know for them at that time, that's what I loved about them. And so, I think Salt-N-Pepa fit in my category of wild, wild women. So, those are the women that pop in my mind. I could probably think of others. But they're also at this intersection of [feminist] politics, music, but also just their aesthetic. I like all of their aesthetics, at least from a fashion perspective, you know. So, I'm also naming that.

In the margin, boxed in with the green gel pen I used that day, is "NAME THAT!" I'm reminded of how Black women are often not afforded the right and privilege to name themselves or even have their names recognized. This has given way to projects such as #sayhername. #Sayhername is part of the long history of Black women's talk-back politics. In explaining why #sayhername was necessary, Kimberlé Crenshaw (executive director of the African American Policy Forum) states:

> Although Black women are routinely killed, raped, and beaten by the police, their experiences are rarely foregrounded in popular understandings of police brutality. Yet, inclusion of Black women's experiences in social movements, media narratives, and policy demands around policing and police brutality is critical to effectively combating racialized state violence for Black communities and other communities of color. (Crenshaw et al. 2015, n.p.)

And so, Black women find themselves creating literacies to name themselves and their experiences (see Garner 2019; Robinson 2019). And by doing so, they offer critiques of society, the way Sekile critiques Black male patriarchy and abuse (both intimate partner abuse and structural abuse) in her reminiscing of Betty Davis. Sekile does the Black feminist work of bringing Black women from the margin to the center through her words and deeds. She sees Black women.

So those are the people who inspire me when I'm shopping for clothes. Like I'm looking for them. I'm looking for clothes [so] I can wear a piece of them, whether it's a bow tie, you know, for Gladys Bentley, or whether it's something sparkly for Diana Ross. You know what I mean? So, I find myself channeling them and being wild. I don't care what's on the rack at Target. I'm wearing some shit from the 1940s. . . . so being wild is also like channeling the energy of people like other wild women. I think having these folks helped me [be brave when I might not have felt brave in the moment]. I can put on their cloak. I can put on my vintage outfit that reminds me of Betty Davis, and I can be wild. If Sekile can't be wild, I can embody Betty Davis. I could channel my inner Betty Davis. Right? If that makes any sense.

Yes, Sekile, that makes sense. We can channel the energies we need to make ourselves whole, allowing us to be wild—wild Black women.

The Interior: A Place Where You Go to Grow Ideas and People

Interior. Let's talk about interior.

So, when you give me words, images pop up.

So, when you gave me wild, Gladys Bentley popped up in my head, and when you gave me interior, I immediately, like, pictured a vulva and a vagina. And so, when I think of interior, I think of strength, and vulnerability, and softness, and desire. And like autonomy, the autonomy to keep it interior or in private and internal or the autonomy to share that interior; that authority to share, to decide what I will share. I think of intimacy and opportunities for connection. Connection back with my body, because, again, I'm channeling. I'm using a vulva as my proxy for interior in this piece. So, I think about it as an opportunity to [*trails off*]. An interior is an opportunity to connect with, getting back in my body, through self-stimulation or to connect with the external world, you know, through another human. So, I guess I think about an interior as a place where you go to grow ideas and people.

In the margin I scribbled, I wish I could draw; need an image. Words do not seem to capture how this part of Sekile's testimony resonated with me, so I thought that an image would be better suited. I imagine a multicolor rendition of a vulva, looking like a sunrise or a galaxy. As I mentioned in chapter 1, sometimes our response to a testimony is to moan, and for me, this image is the form of my moaning.

Sekile weaves a testimony that allows us to cross boundaries, real and imagined, allowing the inside to come out to the exterior by focusing on the individual and yet having that individual be in relation to another and then to the world. We are offered a glimpse into how she is forging an identity, recognizing all parts of her while asserting her sense of self. As I interact with this element of her testimony, I'm reminded of how Audre Lorde (1984), through her writings, has gone in and come out to forge her identity, and we see this when she wrote:

> I was forced to look upon myself and my living with a harsh and urgent clarity that has left me still shaken but much stronger . . . Some of what I experienced during that time has helped elucidate for me much of what I feel concerning the transformation of silence into language and action. . . . In becoming forcibly and essentially aware of my mortality, and

> of what I wished and wanted for my life, however short it might be, priorities and omissions became strongly etched in a merciless light, and what I most regretted were my silences. Of what had I ever been afraid? To question or to speak as I believed could have meant pain, or death. But we all hurt in so many different ways, all the time, and pain will either change or end. Death, on the other hand, is the final silence. And that might be coming quickly, now, without regard for whether I had ever spoken what needed to be said, or had only betrayed myself into small silences, while I planned someday to speak, or waited for someone else's words. And I began to recognize a source of power within myself that comes from the knowledge that while it is most desirable not to be afraid, learning to put fear into a perspective gave me great strength. (x)

For Audre Lorde, the act of speaking, which she intones is political, was forged by going to the interior and dwelling there to access her feelings. This allowed her to understand better how she wanted to be in the world—how she wanted to live her truth. And this is where our power, our erotic, rests.

So, thinking about when I turn inward, that's where my thoughts are coming. When I think about when I gave birth to my children, I had to turn to my interior, like to find the depths of my strength, right, because I had them without medical intervention. And to be able to navigate that pain, physical pain, like you had to tap into, your, you know, your primal. I don't know . . . there was both a disassociation and this grounding in my capacity to do it. The strength that I knew I had to have and that I did have to get that baby out of me. And so, and I had to find it in me. So that's when I think about the interior.

That turn inward. What do we see when we turn inward? Grounding. So, I went. With Cabral, I found out about hypnobirthing through my midwifery practice. One of the midwives did hypnobirthing, and it was learning how to self-hypnotize, learning how to take yourself to this deep state of like interior relaxation where you almost [*trails off*]. And so, there were these affirmations you said daily. Like, I imagine this baby slipping out of me with ease. I imagine my labor being, you know, an enjoyable experience. You would just say these to yourself throughout the day, these affirmations. And it was building up my interior with my strength and my power. But it is also this combination of disembodying yourself, disassociating, but also like associating and actually acknowledging that you had the strength. And so, I think about that interior, that hypnobirthing was part of me tapping into that [*trails off*]. You actually have to practice these prompts and practice what it means to go into yourself, like deeply into yourself, to get this baby out of you, right? But I kept wanting this exterior-like intervention like, "Cedric! I need you to help me get this baby out." He can support me, but he can't get that baby out of me. Only I have the power to get that baby out!

And so, again, I had to stand in that truth and realize, like, oh, I'm these affirmations, [they] are about *me* and what capacity *I* have to get this baby out of me, and how I have to deprogram all the negative thoughts I've heard. Right? So that I could tap into my interior, its depth. And that's what I used to get that baby out. I just went into myself. So, I'm generally a chatty person, but when I'm in pain, I'm super fucking quiet because I am going to the deepest. You do not hear a single sound from me when I'm in labor. I am like I am gone. I am in my head. I am gone. I am in my heart. I am in my body. You know, trying to listen to that baby and listen to what my body needs to do to get that baby out. I don't utter a word when I'm in labor. I don't speak. And so, when I think about interior, that's what it felt like when I go to the deepest parts of my interior. When I'm writing about my blog, and I'm writing, and I'm unearthing all that shit that I haven't had a chance to speak about, you know, that's interior for me, too, like going deep to my depths [of trauma.]

Me and my capacity *allow me to find*
Grounding,
That turn inward
And so, I went deep inside me
Going deep to my depth
Finding it in me
But I had to
Go *[to]* my deepest
In my head
In my body
In my heart

I read these words and eventually realized that tears are pooling in my eyes. I don't have an explanation. But sometimes, testimonies hit us in places and in ways that are not easily understood using a Western philosophic understanding of knowing/knowledge. Something else happens when I read these words, I engage in what I can only call a "praise dance." Finally, after this happened on more than one occasion, it came to me that the ancestors were visiting through Sekile's testimony. And so, I stopped fighting it and allowed myself to be in community with not just Sekile's testimony, but also the testimony of the ancestors—those Black women of whom I am a part of their lineage, the ones who were not seen or heard in their quest for justice, the ones Audre Lorde told me to listen to. The tears and the praise dance were needed to engage this testimony.

And I think of the work of Ntozake Shange (1997) and how she used physicality, language, and movement, inviting us to find god in ourselves. Shange shows us how the Black body, the Black female body, becomes a knowledge repository. And that this knowledge is not simply individual but represents collective knowledge. As such, the Black female moving body is a compilation of historical narratives/texts that are available for us to tap into as we navigate life. Thus, my praise dance.

My Relationships Are Divine

Divine. What comes to mind?

So, this will be kind of mushy, but I'm finding it divine to be like in a woman's bosom. Like there's just something soft and luscious about that, like being cuddled up with a woman and [*trails off*]. Particularly those who are similar to us—I guess I think I do have a bias towards curvier women because I immediately imagined [*trails off*]. Well, you know, I definitely have been with a woman who has like a small bust, and I can't say that her body's popping up in my head. So, I hate to be horrible [*trails off*].

"It is what it is!" I said in the moment of our testimonial session. Later I went back to Audre Lorde, and I read "the sharing of joy, whether physical, emotional, psychic, or intellectual," that embraces the entire body, that "flows through and colors . . . life with a kind of energy that heightens and sensitizes and strengthens all . . . experience" *(Lorde 1984, 56). This is what Sekile is expressing—how she shares joy and her capacity to share joy.*

I know we're not supposed to have these interpretations. You're supposed to be body neutral. But I guess in my mind, I'm picturing . . . there's something just divine about being with a woman who's similarly navigating the world. So, I'm thinking about a woman I'm dating right now, and she's a mom just like me, and so she's trying to make it just like me, we just started dating. And I remember last Friday, I was going over to her house, and I was thinking, I just want to lay on the couch and cuddle because it's just been a week. And when I got there, I was like, you want to? She was like, "I just want to lay down and cuddle," and I was like, "I had the same exact thought." And so, because I think there's also this way in which we're always caring for others. There's something interesting in that you got two people who do the same thing for everyone else, and now you actually have someone doing that for you and with, you know . . . just like laying, cuddling, it feels divine like you know, [*to*] be wrapped in care. And because I think particularly as caregivers, that's not something that we get, like just you know, this mutual, nonhierarchical form of care. Right? And so, we're being cared for and nurtured, and it's actually reciprocal. And so, having that reciprocity, that feels divine—[*brief interruption*].

Nonhierarchical form of care? When is the last time I experienced that?

Naming desires.

Reciprocity

Friendships as a spiritual place. bell hooks on healing—Sisters of the Yam is the note that is scribbled hurriedly in the margin as I want to be fully present in Sekile's testimony. hooks comes to mind as she speaks of healing spaces and how that can occur in community. Specifically, hooks (1993, 6) tells us that yams are a "life-sustaining symbol of Black kinship and community." *Using yams as a symbol, hooks asserts that the yam symbolizes Black women's diasporic connections and friendships. And we see how Sekile is nourished by "yams" in a way that helps her to (re)create self in her own image.*

Sekile lays bare the complex and intricate relationships Black girls and women can have with their families. As a way of working through Sekile's testimony, once again, I turn to bell hooks (2000a)

> When we understand love as the will to nurture our own, and another's spiritual growth, it becomes clear that we cannot claim to love if we are hurtful and abusive. Love and abuse cannot coexist. Abuse and neglect are, by definition, the opposites of nurturance. and care. . . . An overwhelming majority of us come from dysfunctional families in which we were taught that we were not okay, where we were shamed, verbally and/or physically abused, and emotionally neglected even as we were also taught to believe that we were loved. For most folks, it is just too threatening to embrace a definition of love that would no longer enable us to see love as present in our

> families. Too many of us need to cling to a notion of love that either makes abuse acceptable or at least makes it seem that whatever happened was not that bad. (6)

Sekile, like hooks, recognizes the harm caused by those who are supposed to nurture and nourish, yet she talks back. And this is probably why I see the color red as I sat with how to engage her testimony. Red represents death and power. As I read and reread Sekile's testimony, I see both. Death that happens at the hands of abusers and the exercise of power to allow that structure of being to die so that one, Sekile, can live in her power.

And then there is "there's something just divine about being with a woman who's similarly navigating the world." *As part of her articulation of self, it is evident that it is essential for Sekile to find and define her community by those who can understand and appreciate the spectrum of her experiences. In these communities, her "yams," Sekile is able to find a "home."* In talking about home, hooks (1989b) asserts,

> [It] is no longer just one place. It is locations. Home is that place which enables and promotes varied and everchanging perspectives, a place where one discovers new ways of seeing reality, frontiers of difference. One confronts and accepts dispersal, fragmentation as part of the construction of a new world order that reveals more fully where we are, who we can become, an order that does not demand forgetting. (19)

So, then I think of divine in a nonsexual space like when you're just with your girlfriends, your platonic girlfriends, too. So that's a divine connection, where everyone's just catching each other. I feel like my friendships are divine for me. It's the way in which I re-created family. And when I've had the absence of family, and it's interesting because folks, queer and trans folks have articulated, you know, how they've had to reconstruct family. Black folks also talk about that tradition of having our families broken apart from [being captured in] Africa [and through our] enslavement. Right? Or our families being [torn apart] [*trails off*] and so how we've always just kind of reimagine notions of family.

Friendships can offer the possibility for re-creating families and, in so doing, provide a method of managing disembodiment by allowing those involved to tap into their interior. Friendships can provide us with the type of intimacy, sexual and nonsexual, that allows us to go deeper into our-

selves, especially if they are not couched in a capitalist patriarchal system, as suggested by Lorde, which brings me to Ntozake Shange's choreopoem, For Colored Girls Who Have Considered Suicide/When the Rainbow Is Enuf. *In this work, Shange represents the fluidity of the "self"/"I" by placing it in relation to others, thereby allowing the "self"/"I" to be transformed through community.*

In the choreopoem, the Lady in Brown sings, "can't hear anything/ but maddening screams & the soft strains of death" *(Shange 1997, 4). She has been locked, at least metaphorically, in silence. And by singing of how she can't even hear herself and is possibly not heard or seen by others, the Lady in Brown brings attention to how Black women are often made invisible. However, as she sings, the other women surround her, standing in silence, thus, giving her the space to be heard, especially by herself. Sekile's friendships, across women of various backgrounds and in various capacities, allow her to hear—to hear herself.*

[A less talked about] group is those of us who have trauma histories, particularly sexual violence if it's been in our birth families. Right? We've also had to reimagine what family has looked like because going home isn't safe, right. For many trans, nonbinary folks, [*and*] queer folks, home is not safe. And many people who are navigating child sexual abuse, unfortunately, are not safe at home either. The reality of [unsafe] homes, which has been really a triggering thing for me as I think about COVID. I thought about all the [school-aged] kids right now, who are at home and all the college students who are having to go back home and how that neither one of those, K through 12, even through college, that wouldn't have been a safe [situation.] That just wouldn't been a safe option for me.

And so those [*pause*] my divine spaces have been [my chosen] family—the families that I have created, which have largely been women, you know Black women, women of color, [feminists]. I mean, they've been all kinds of women. . . . But I would yeah, I would say women whom I can connect with, that's been divine for me to be in their arms, right. So, I imagine myself also in their bosom, but in this version, the image, the person has clothes on, right! [*laughter*]. I kind of make those distinctions between my intimate partners that I'm having sexual relationships with, and I also define these folks as my intimate partners who are, I would argue, like my sisters. I want to have different kinds of boundaries [and notions of intimacy.] So yeah, that's divine for me. My relationships are divine.

"That's beautiful. Makes sense to me." I said this while we were recording this testimony. And as I read and reread Sekile's testimony, I find myself

crying. It seems that the tears that have sat in the bottom of the place were tears are collected and gathered opened up. I, too, have students who cannot go home or whose home is dangerous. It was only as I engaged Sekile's testimony did I allow the fear that I have been feeling for these students to come forth. It is as if I have been too afraid to let myself go to that place inside of me, to tap into those fears and express them because I feared that I would lose control. So here we get back to this issue of control and how it can limit us from feeling and feeling deeply. Control can take us outside of the sensuality that gives our lives texture. And Sekile reminds me that it is okay to go to those places even if the texture is rough to the touch.

And all of this pools into me. And I think of how Black women experience mourning and how we are allowed to mourn. I often say that Black women are in a constant state of mourning given the race-gender violences we face both directly and indirectly. But often, we are not afforded space to mourn. We mourn us—and what we lose because of violence, directly and indirectly, we are forced to experience. I remember, for example, when Trayvon Martin was murdered and the type of deep mourning I experienced. One day as I sat, it came to me that I was mourning a child that I'd lost in a similar manner. It was not my child in this current moment, it was a child that I'd given life to in another lifetime/period as I/he was part of the lineage of Black women who face such violence. I needed to sit in the company of these women, the ancestors, to fully understand and recognize the depth of my mourning. When we are in the company of women, as Sekile speaks of, maybe, just maybe, we can be heard and seen, and our mourning can happen.

Feminine: Grounded in Hardness and Strength

Now for the word feminine.

For me, [*pause*] that's a hard one.

We can come back

Yeah. No. I think [*pause*]. I think hardness is showing up for me when I think about it. And I don't know why hardness is like a [*trails off as she pops her gum*]. Well, because I think my softness always has like a hard edge, I think I want to name softness, but I want to name like the hard edge that I [*slight pause*] that I need to accompany my softness within it. And I'm not even defining that as masculinity. I just don't want to. That's not gender for me. But there is [an] edge that I need to my femininity for it to have meaning for me. What it means to be feminine for me has to be grounded in hardness and strength, and power.

Duality, how duality shows up in our interior, is something that I sense Sekile is expressing. Yet, we are often limited in expressing this duality as it is often not given space to exist. For example, some of us are told to choose to be wild or good, that we cannot simultaneously be both. And this is the tension that I hear in Sekile's testimony. Hardness alongside softness cannot exist. This is probably what prompted Audre Lorde to often self-define herself in a particular way, a desire to resist binaries by recognizing the ANDS of our existence (see Lorde 1982).

And, it can have a little playfulness in it and a little like [*trails off*]. I don't know, a little bit of surprise. I don't know what I'm trying to say. I feel like there's a way I talk about fashion and the way I dress at work. I wear a lot of vintage. So, a lot of my clothing could present to others [*switches thought*]. If you don't know me, you could think I'm actually a conservative person. Right. Because if you look at what . . . I wear a lot of pussy bow blouses and a skirt. But I wear pussy bows because I just love them, and I love that I get to be naughty and actually say pussy bow blouse [in the office.] So, nobody knows that [*laughter*]. But it's me like being intentionally provocative without people knowing. I wear a skirt not because I'm super feminine; I wear a skirt because it's easier for me than wearing pants [with these thick thighs.] I wear dresses [*trails off*]. I can just pull it up if I want to fuck, right? I'm just being honest [*laughter*].

But if someone reads me, they're like, oh, she has on this pussy bow blouse and the skirt. And so, there's the way in which I know I'm being misinterpreted/[misread]. Right. And so, the joke is on them; I guess if you will, right? The joke is on them: I'm wearing something that you think I'm wearing it for one reason.

How do we begin to color outside the lines? Sekile suggests a kind of inversion—taking what means one thing and using it for another purpose. Like the way she speaks of why she wears dresses and skirts—for one, it's just easier for her to engage in sexual activity. I laugh at this. And then I reflect on why I tend to wear pants—beyond the fact that I've always loved pants from early childhood. But there is another reason why I tend to wear pants, and that is because it is my way of managing the male gaze—one that saw me as a sexual object since I was about ten years old.

I can vividly remember walking and men commenting on my body, and I thought that those unwanted comments would end if I just covered it up. It started when I was walking in Bridgetown (the central city in Barbados with my father). I was wearing a pair of green culottes/pedal pushers. They were my favorite, and so I can remember them vividly. I also remember this experience as I rarely went into town with my father. I cannot remember the purpose of our trip, but some parts of that trip simply stay in my memory. We were in Lower Broad Street, the main street, heading back to the car park. We had just made it past Collins (a store), and this man, walking in the opposite direction, said, "I could eat that pussy!" I sensed my father tensing up, and he declared, "What did you just say?" I mumbled, "Dad, come on." We never spoke of that incident. But it lingered. And I learned to cover up, to play within certain lines as a way of protecting myself.

And Sekile shows me how she uses her voice, vis-à-vis her clothing, to engage in resistance. bell hooks, in speaking of being on the margins, tells us that this position is "much more than a site of deprivation [. . .] it is also the site of radical possibility, a space of resistance" for the "oppressed, exploited and colonized people" (1989a, 341–42). *Marginality affords us, at least some of us, the possibility of engaging in counternarratives. These counternarratives can then serve as the voice, or a voice, that constitutes critical consciousness. Critical consciousness is what is needed to tap into the interior. And I find myself going into my interior and thinking of my ten-year-old self. I did not know about oral sex and could not begin to process what this man meant when he said what he said. But that has traveled with me and has influenced how I live my truth and the lines I "play" within. Sekile's testimony gave me an opening to think of how I can reimagine a different response—after all, I have been covering up for forty years.*

But what I've been struggling with is respectability politics. Because I had a Black woman, queer woman, a grad student who dressed in a way that might be read to others that she was a sex worker like she wore short shorts, she [wore colorful and long] wigs, and she would sometimes wear her short shorts with fishnet stockings or high-heeled boots. She was one of our PhD students in African American studies, and she was [viewed as] provocative in another way [through her clothing]. She and I, I think both use [clothes]—but what happens is people will have a higher tolerance for me because of how they read my body [and presentation of Black femininity] and a dismissal or erasure of hers.

So, I've been struggling with my self-presentation around what it means to have this kind of respectable presentation of femininity and how that undermines other Black women's expressions of their femininity. You know, so like just respectability politics. I'm not trying to play respectability [*politics*]. I'm actually poking fun at them in many ways.

Right. But you only know that if you're in my head. Or so I think, or in my bed [*laughter*]. So, I think that I've been playing around, thinking about that. So yeah, I think I am intentionally now, maybe I'm wearing a possible pussy bow blouse on one day, and maybe I'm wearing a shirt with cleavage another day. Right! And being okay. There's a whole thing about [so-called] work cleavage. And so, me and my [sex positive feminist] friends joke about it. We're like, yeah, I got my work cleavage showing today. And it's intentional to be disruptive of what's known as professionalism [and modesty].

So, when I think about feminine, I think about all of that like it's still . . . it's a performance, and it's a way for me to mind fuck you around what you think my feminine is. So that's what I mean about that edge and that it is also an [subversive] intellectual and political performance for me, too, because I also think when white folks see me walk in with a suit on and a button-down shirt and [*slight pause*], it's vintage they're reading it like, oh, this is a respectable Black woman. And so, then I like to open my mouth and spitfire. Right. And so that they're reading me as conservative because I'm conservatively dressed, but I'm anything but [*laughter*]. And so I like to be disruptive; I like my feminine energy to catch them off guard or my feminine representation, feminized representation to catch them off guard.

In her engagement with Black women's respectability politics, Brittney Cooper (2018, 21) writes, "race women took it as their political and intellectual work to give shape and meaning to the Black body in social and political terms, to make it legible as an entity with infinite value and social worth." *Black women entering public spaces are often required to perform in a particular way, and a failure to do such can result in real consequences, including death, for example. Black women are often not welcomed in the world in all of our Blackness and womanness, and so, Sekile has found a way to return the gaze, calling into question what the "norm" means. The sensuousness of her actions is more than just a fashion statement. Instead, it is a lush language of voice and resistance. Her clothing choices act as a mobilizing force, allowing Sekile to challenge lines, lines that often tell wild Black girls to "sit their wild behinds down," to be seen and not heard. This is what I argue Lorde was speaking to when she states,* "There are many kinds of power." *But that power can be hidden, diluted, and beaten out of us with expectations that we follow the line—the patriarchal, gender, racial, and class lines. Yet, we can subvert it, and the way to subvert is to come into the erotic.*

Energy: Something I Read

Now let's turn to energy.

Yeah, I feel like I when I think about energy, I think about the way I read the world or read others like I read people's energy so I can tell [*laughter*] if I'm gonna fuck with you or not. I can tell, and I've been wrong, but I'm usually not. I think about energy as something I assess. It is something that I read, and I read the energy in the room. I read the [environment] and people, and I decide how to enter into that space or relationship based on energy. The way I read energy, I decide how much energy I'm going to put into something, so based on other people's energy. So, you know, universities performing around how they're committed to social justice is bullshit. Right! So, I already know that I'm going to perform, that I'm going to know I'm going to do the bare minimum. But I'm not going to give it my actual energy like you're getting. A performance, so my energy comes through performance, not through genuine, authentic expression of my capacity, my interest, or my ability.

So, energy is also something I assign to work, which was really why I was able to come back to higher [education], because when I came back, I was like, oh, this is your job. This is not who you are. Leaving allowed me to develop a clear articulation of who I was because I think, you know, sometimes it's hard. Like our jobs become us, and they become our identities. And so, I had to remember, oh, a professor is what you do. It's not who you are. Right!

"A performance, so the energy comes through performance, not through genuine, authentic expression of my capacity, my interest, my ability." *As I read this, I'm reminded of Audre Lorde's engagement with learning to write her name (see chapter 1) and how, in the telling of that experience, she centers the notion of performance and how it necessitates a betrayal—a betrayal of self. And so, the tenor of our lives become less deep and full. And at times, we have to create fictive landscapes that allow our passions for our truth to be nourished and fortified. Thereby moving us outside of the lines designed to hold us in. Then we meet our authentic selves. This is how Black women manage betrayal and the disembodiment that can result—we go to the interior, and we make it real. In the interior, we make ourselves real using the feelings that reside there.*

I say this to my staff all the time. Make sure you're doing political work outside of your job. Do not expect to have your political intentions manifest in this workplace. [*In the initial interview, Sekile mentioned a conversation with an individual, and although no name was mentioned, Sekile redacted this part of the conversation to protect them.*] [I say] this is not political work. This is a job. These are two different [things], you know. So, my political home is Chicago Abortion Fund. And of course, I'm connected to other [movement work but this] is where I'm putting my full energy. I will stay up at two o'clock in the morning working on something for the Chicago Abortion Fund because that's where I want to put my energy. I have never in three years been up at two o'clock working on anything for Northwestern.

I'm real committed to where I put my energy. And so that is what's kept me whole. The only thing that's been compromised since I've been in the interim CDO role because people pull on your energy differently, and I haven't been able to keep up. And so, they require me to be in that performance space [at higher levels], which takes me away from the things I'm committed to. But it was my therapist and I who got clear about that. They asked, "Do you want to keep giving them that energy?" And I was like, Nah. So, they said, "OK, we're going to say thank you, but no, thank you. We're not applying to this full-time position."

Audre Lorde (1984) writes,

> I am responsible for educating teachers who dismiss my children's culture in school. Black and Third World people are expected to educate white people as to our humanity. Women are expected to educate men. Lesbians and gay men are expected to educate the heterosexual world. (114–115)

And Lorde goes on to question the merit of these "educational projects," showing how they move us, particularly the ones having to do the teaching, away from our erotic as they are simply performative tasks. Furthermore, Lorde argues that these performative tasks actually work to maintain the power status quo. Consider that "The oppressors maintain their position and evade responsibility for their own actions" (115). *As a result,* "there is a constant drain of energy which might be better used in redefining ourselves and devising realistic scenarios for altering the present and constructing the future" (115). *By reading the room and determining where to put her energy, Sekile challenges the status quo.*

And so that was about [clarifying] where I wanted to put my energy. I have not been able to do my work with the reproductive justice. You know, I haven't been doing my movement work as much, and I miss it terribly. And so that's where I want to put my energy. I had to just kind of remember that truth.

"Right, right, right. So, tell me about your movement work, and what drew you to that, what allows you to determine that's where you want to put your energy? What is it about that, what is it about the Chicago Abortion Fund that draws you, that keeps you up at two o'clock at night doing that work?"

One way I can approach it is when I'm prepping for class. Say I'm teaching an intro class where it's like a survey class, you got to cover everything. There are sections where you definitely need your notes, you definitely need your PowerPoint, you know the broad strokes, but you're definitely going to need your notes in the sections that are not yours. But you can go up there for two hours straight with no notes [when you know and love] your shit. You know, you know the histories, you know the work. It's in you in a different way.

This is wealth building. I think of wealth beyond money or even the collection of tangible things. Wealth to me means the collection of knowledge—the type of knowledge that is important for justice work. Wealth also means consciousness raising—individual and communal. This is Ashiakle in action. And this way of approaching work signifies how Sekile talks back against a system that seeks to "corrupt" our work. We are cautioned, by Audre Lorde (1984), that

> The principal horror of any system which defines the good in terms of profit rather than in terms of human need, or which defines human need to the exclusion of the psychic and emotional components of that need—the principal horror of such a system is that it robs our work of its erotic value. Such a system reduces work to a travesty of necessities, a duty by which we earn bread or oblivion for ourselves and those we love. But this is tantamount to blinding a painter and then telling her to improve her work, and to enjoy the act of painting. It is not only next to impossible, it is also profoundly cruel. (55)

The sanctioned way of being can take us away from ourselves and each other as it creates competitiveness and constant pressure to produce, and often outside of our erotic as our work is emptied of the spiritual, sensual, and political. Like Lorde, Sekile is talking back to neoliberal political, socioeconomic structures that seek to control and punish while promoting individualism; thus, making work devoid of the erotic.

And that's how I feel about my RJ [reproduction justice] stuff, and even messing around sex, sexual violence, and healing from that; there's a way in which I notice myself when I'm talking in front of a crowd. There's no nerves. The world just drops away, and it comes into focus at the same time. Right. And there's a way in which I am fearless, and I am connected to humanity in a way that it does not feel like work, it feels like this is what I was, it feels like my purpose like this is why I'm here. This is why I'm here! And so, and I can tell when I'm in front, or even when I'm behind the scenes, because, like I said, I'm doing something till two o'clock in the morning, and my name's not even going on it. I don't even care. Like, I'm not trying to get credit for it. I never sit and be like, OK, let me update my CV. That's not why I'm doing it, right.

It's me getting off a plane and looking at my phone, and it's someone from Chicago Abortion Fund saying, hey, we've got a woman coming in from Louisiana who flew into Chicago for an abortion, and she's never flown before [*trails off*]. Can anyone get to the airport to get her to help her get to her appointment? And I'm taxiing, right? Only the universe does that. I'm literally taxiing into the airport that they're sending a note, hey, we got somebody, and I'm like, I can get her. I can get her. Now, here's the thing. The night before, the day before, my flights got canceled over and over and over; they kept getting delayed, delayed, delayed, then canceled. And I had to stay overnight. It was coming to Chicago, and it took us to Detroit, and I had to stay overnight in fucking Detroit. And I ended up getting on the next flight the next morning. Only the universe does that.

I was supposed to be in Chicago the day before. And then I get a text [*trails off*]. I'm taxiing as this woman who's scared, you know, is coming and is in her second trimester and can't get an abortion in Louisiana and navigating domestic violence. I mean, her face is fractured from her boyfriend punching her in her face. Right. She's pregnant. She's got two babies at home. She's got hypothyroidism, and she's a sista. And so, I've [*trails off*]. And her phone can't hold a charge because he smashed her phone. And so, she's trying to tell me where she is in the airport. Right. And I'm trying to find her. And I'm like, oh, just meet me in baggage claim because I'm talking like someone who knows airports. I'm not realizing she's never been to an airport before. So, saying something like, oh, meet me [at baggage claim], and she doesn't translate, and then her phone dies.

Right. And so, it's taking me forever to find [her]. And I finally realized I should have told her to stand still, and I should have gotten her. Eventually, she's coming down the escalator, and I see her and, and I, and I look at her, and she just crumbles, and she's just crying, and I just hold her.

We don't know each other. And I told her, I said, "It's going to be OK. You're going to be fine. It's going to be OK." It's going to be OK. Right. And we got you. [*She pops her gum.*] We got you. And so, this is our underground railroad; we get them, we care for these sisters [*who*] come in from wherever they're coming from. Over 50 percent of the people getting abortions right now are going out of state, and we are trying to support them. This is like reproductive terrorism; since Trump has come into power, it is just so unsafe. It is unsafe for folks to get an abortion [in this hostile climate]. And so, and of course, it's unsafe to raise children [in this hostile climate]. I mean, the whole reproductive spectrum and our lives are under attack.

REPRODUCTIVE TERRORISM

Black women are constantly under threat. A famous quote circulated on social media says, "We were never meant to survive." They quote from Audre Lorde's poem "Litany of Survival." This poem shows that some of us are simply never afforded the luxury of safety. Furthermore, Lorde shows how this terrorism, birthed from race, gender, capitalism, and patriarchy, haunts as it follows marginalized bodies from childhood through adulthood and is also generational. While recognizing the fear that comes from constantly being under threat, Lorde intones, "So it is better to speak / remembering / we were never meant to survive."

"Yaas! SPEAK That!"

(This is my response to Sekile's testimony in the moment.)

But this is what I've been calling reproductive terrorism as I watch this woman [and so many others] just being terrorized, right? You know, and she tried to get her tubes tied, and in the state of fucking Louisiana because she wasn't twenty-one, they wouldn't because she hadn't had three kids yet. So, here's the other thing right there, it's an anti-choice state with religious zealots in power. There, she could not get her tubes tied. And so, she tried to get it after [her] first baby, and her doctor wouldn't get let her tie her tubes. So just controlling her reproduction on the other end, too. And she's telling me, I'm going to get pregnant again. She's like, he's going to. He doesn't use [*trails off*]. "I can't make him use a condom." So, also just her navigating, knowing that this is her truth. This is her truth. Right!

The universe tells me where I'm supposed to be. I was tired. I was tired, you know. I had spent the whole day in the airport and, you know, trying to get home from Atlanta. I had cut up all weekend with my friends. So, I was tired, but yeah, I had energy for that.

She pops her gum and stares off into the distance. The brief moment of silence seems necessary for this part of her testimony. And so, I sit listening to the popping until she is ready to resume.

I think for me, it's that I can see past myself. I can see past institutions, past laws, and know that I'm just supposed to show up for people and that they show up for me. And so yes, so I think that movement work is really like a politic for me that is deeply personal, but also, I don't know, I think it's just not about me, it's like it's just, you know, it's just what needs to happen, right!

You know, that's why [when Chicago Abortion Fund says], [we're bringing them to our homes to care for them if needed] [*shifts thought and Sekile redacted some information that preceded next thought*] . . . here's me like in my class shit that I, we, don't like to acknowledge. Like we talk about race and gender all the time, and we don't like to acknowledge our [middle] class shit that we've internalized. [When I found her at the airport, I asked,] "Do you want something to eat?" There was a Starbucks right there at the baggage claim. And I asked if she wanted something from Starbucks. I didn't think. And then I realized—like oh shit, Sekile, you know you done been around these middle-class people so long, your ass [*shifts thought*] you're making an assumption that everybody [fucks with] Starbucks. Right. So, I had to catch myself. And so, I was like, what would you like to eat? And she was like, "I would like some McDonald's." And I was like, "OK, we're going to get you some McDonald's!" When we got to my house, she showered because, you know, she's [boldly] escaping [her circumstance]. And while she showered, I went and got McDonald's, and we just sat at my table and talked [like new old friends].

The crescent moon brings us growth. And Sekile shows us how consciousness allows us to grow so that we can work across differences in our quest for justice. In Shadow Bodies *(2017), I speak to how some Black women become shadows in other Black women's larger organizing and activism efforts. They are present but never fully in view, so their needs are never fully addressed vis-à-vis policy or how the policy issue is defined. Sekile speaks to this type of intragroup intersectionality by interrogating class differences. In doing so, this sister is allowed to be seen.* "Institutionalized rejection of difference is an absolute necessity in a profit economy which needs outsiders as surplus people" *(Lorde 1984, 115). And rejection of difference can happen between races and genders and between those of the same race and gender. This is what I mean by intragroup intersectionality (see Jordan-Zachery 2017). Class can be a proxy through which* "institutionalized rejection" *can occur. Regina Austin (1992) posits,*

> It may be time to recognize that the only true communities of black females are voluntary associations of women who are bound by shared economic, political, and social constraints and find strength, economic support, and moral guidance through affective, face-to-face engagement with each other. Such an admission would interfere with our nostalgic longing for a not too distant past when success nationally obviated the need to come together locally, as well as highlight our reluctance to analyze the contemporary material landscape and the full extent of the class cleavages that separate black women. The enormous comfort that comes from being able to think, talk, and act in terms of their being a "black community" or a "black sisterhood" would be threatened if we called core assumptions into question. Dare we? (887)

I'm reminded of how Sekile speaks of reciprocity, and we see how she engages in reciprocity by daring to see across differences. Furthermore, we see how Sekile rejects the corruption of the erotic that Lorde cautions against. Lorde suggests that the corruption of the erotic takes place when we are unable to see others and their truths. When we engage the erotic in the "good" we do, then we are able to experience "deep participation" *that takes place outside of the* "abuse of feeling" *with each other (Lorde 1984, 57).*

And then I handed her off. [*Sekile redacted this part.*] But when my girl dropped her off, she was like, *yo, I didn't like the way that woman received her*. She gave her some book and said, please, when you feel rested, share your story about your abortion. And she was like, we don't, we never ask them for their stories. They can share their stories if they want to. But to make that a condition after you just open your home to her makes it feel obligatory. And so, then she also had a pull-out couch. Now, this woman has been crying nonstop. She didn't feel comfortable and was of the mindset of where can I go and just cry? Right. And then she's never left the state of Louisiana. So, the woman goes to work and leaves her, and the thing is, we have to, like, actually be caring for these people, they're coming to us in crisis. So, some may need alone time, and some may need you to be with them. And you have to be able to, if we say we're here for them, we have to be able to [be there].

So, we're like, okay, you know, we're getting her a hotel room. We're just like, fuck it. We don't feel good on this one. We get her a room, and then we developed a meal train. We found out she smoked cigarettes. So, this is what it means to be judgment-free, right? Because she's pregnant. Somebody could be like, oh, she's not—fuck that. She is stressed the fuck out. She has been beaten and just got off a plane for the first time! This woman is brave! We ain't judging her because she wants to smoke cigarettes. And we're just kind of like, what does it mean to really just center *her* in this moment?

What does it mean to center a sista in a moment? What does it mean for Black women to see each other? Sekile offers us one example of how we can hold each other tenderly.

And to care for her. And that's what movement work is. It isn't—for me—you'll rarely see me at a protest. I was at Chicago Abortion Fund for six years. I got on the mic in year seven. I never was in front. I was petrified when I did. I generally just did the work. I'm not on CNN. That's not what movement work is to me, quite honestly. I'm not a superstar activist. I'm just whatever; I don't even know. I wouldn't even say I'm an activist. I just know that I'm committed to this work and our collective humanity.

I moan. I let Sekile's testimony stand on its own. The care she offers needs nothing but a moan.

Erotic: A Joy Space

Tell me about erotic.

So, dancing comes to mind for me.

Dancing is my erotic space that I know, and sometimes I forget. I know that I loved dancing my whole childhood. I danced in middle school. I danced in high school. I danced in college. And I wanted to be a dancer when I grew up. But I had a lot of people shoot that down when I was growing up. And so, I think I always treated it like a hobby or like an extracurricular thing, but I never committed to it as a career because I was just discouraged from [it]. But it is a joy space for me. I remember [*trails off*]. Yeah, dancing, it can, it can get me into trouble [*laughter*].

"We gotta dance to keep from crying/we gotta dance to keep from dying" (Shange 1997, 15). *So yes, Sekile dance! I think of my mother's love for dancing and the freedom she experiences when she gets lost in the music. She often shared how music always makes her feel "so good," and a smile would light up her face.*

As you talk about being erotic because I think it is where I feel like embodied, and I feel sexy, and again, it's like these places where the world just falls away, and it comes into focus at the same time. And it's just like and I can . . . I can feel myself connecting with myself and connecting with people across the room. So, I remember in high school and in college, I would be dancing with a guy. And if that guy could dance, he was getting it! It was going to happen! The guys I had crushes on, the guys I dated, were always guys who could dance, you know. And I remember actually, even when Cedric and I were had just gotten engaged and we went to study abroad to Ghana, and we had to do African dance classes for several days as part of our study abroad. And, of course, the guys didn't want to dance. It was mostly Black guys, too. But Cedric was hanging in there with them classes. And I remember thinking, like, yeah, I see you. And I was like, really impressed by that. But [*trails off*] and it's been a point of departure for us, too, because when he goes out, he likes to go out to bars and like maybe sit and have drinks and listen to music. And I, as soon as I walk in the door, I'm like beeline to the dance floor. He's like, can I get a drink first!? And I'm just like, I want to dance now!

So, when I first got married, I felt really constrained. My erotic [was] constrained in some ways because I knew that the dance floor brought out a particular erotic energy in me, and I couldn't figure out how to navigate that now that I was married, so I just stopped dancing. I stopped going out to clubs because I didn't want to get in trouble. I thought I'm definitely cheat on this guy if I go out dancing. So, I couldn't figure out how to channel this erotic component of me to be in this [monogamous] marriage. So, I stopped and then it was sad because he was a good dancer, we enjoyed dancing, but it wasn't like part of our relationship like a thing we did, you know, with kids and careers. We hardly get to do anything fun given our full lives, you know. So, I just stopped dancing and going out dancing.

"What are the tyrannies you swallow day by day and attempt to make your own, until you will sicken and die of them, still in silence? We have been socialized to respect fear more than our own need for language" (Lorde 2017, 3). *I reflect on how my mother tells of her love of dance and my father's reticence. When they got married in 1969 my mother would go to parties with her male cousin as this was not something my dad wanted to do. Eventually, she stopped because of what others would say. She started to play within the lines. Putting down her own desires, the sensuality felt by dancing. And I'm not suggesting that my mother was without agency, but I also recognize how her decision was constrained by societal norms of how a good wife behaved. Audre Lorde warns us that the erotic, beyond the sexual, is feared by a capitalist, patriarchal, sexist society. However, instead of managing its/their own fears, those in power tend to structure society in a way that lessens our willingness and ability to tap into our erotic. A good wife was not seen with another man, even if her cousin, and could not enjoy a good dance unless accompanied by her husband, or she ran the risk of being cast as loose—the wild woman. Eventually, I became her dance partner. As a little girl, she and I would dance around the house for hours. As an adult, I find myself wondering what my mother's life would have been like if she were able to dance with her peers. Sara Ahmed (2015), in thinking through how we respond to pain, invites us not to fetishize suffering, but instead to be open to interpreting it in relation to the structures that caused the pain. Then we can move into action. I read Lorde's "Uses of the Erotic" in the same way; it is not a call to fetishize pain but to recognize how our experiences are influenced by structures that can be very oppressive and move us beyond our erotic. And this is the context within which I now reflect on my mother's and Sekile's decision to constrain themselves from what brought them pleasure.*

And so, since we opened up, I have been going out with friends to dance, to party like in mostly queer spaces, but just to party [*trails off*]. Last summer was probably the first time I started. It might have been like two or three times. But I remember having so much fun, and I remembered this is my erotic space. I felt like I could lean into that joy because it didn't feel like I was cheating on my partner [*laughter*].

And so, I feel like my erotic, to be honest, has been suppressed because I'm not dancing. So that's been suppressed for a real long time, you know. I didn't know it until it was reawakened recently, you know. Just this January, I went to this party for queer women, and I was super nervous at first. I'm super shy [as a late bloomer]. As I as I've come out, it feels, I feel kind of like what a fourteen-year-old boy feels like at the school dance, too scared to ask somebody to dance. But also super horny and thinking every girl's cute. That's kind of how I describe my [entry into my queerness]. I feel very much like a teen. [Like] a teenager must feel like—hormonal. Hormones rushing through bumbling, awkward dialogues [*trails off*].

She stops speaking and burst out laughing. Then she simply pops her gum with her eyes averted from the camera. But the joy is contagious. And to be honest, it feels liberatory. When Sekile laughs, I see how she is channeling her inner "B-girl," the one who recognizes the limits and also decides to "perform" to show her understanding of self.

Her naming of her sexual desires and longings is received as a sacred calling to return to self and an imagining of a future where her full self is recognized and embraced. Thus, I read this as an attempt to engage in the act of creative and material justice-filled world-building.

So, I went to this party, and after several drinks, [filled] with liquid courage, I started being able to finally dance. I started dancing with people, and I started enjoying myself, and then all of a sudden, it didn't even matter. I didn't even need people. And I found myself just dancing by myself. And I got lost in myself. At one point, I remembered that I was supposed to be meeting people! Like I just was enjoying myself so much.

And I think I remembered it like, oh, you enjoy dancing! This is your vibe. Actually, I said I was going to meet people, but the music was what I needed more than the connection to other people. And it was just like I just danced all night. I'm telling you; my legs were sore the next day [*switches thought*], and I wasn't dancing with other people. I literally forgot the point of the evening, which was to meet women, like it's just dancing [to] the music, the deejay was good, and I just could not stop dancing. I just stayed on the floor under this, disco ball for hours.

More joyous laughter. The laughter is as important to Sekile's testimony as her words. In a way, her laugh is a signifier of how she talks back to power. In writing about marginality, hooks (1990) asserts that marginality is

> much more than a site of deprivation; in fact I was saying just the opposite, that it is also the site of radical possibility, a space of resistance. It was this marginality that I was naming as a central location for the production of a counter-hegemonic discourse that is not just found in words but in habits of being and the way one lives. As such, I was not speaking of a marginality one wishes to lose—to give up or surrender as part of moving into the center—but rather of a site one stays in, clings to even, because it nourishes one's capacity to resist. It offers to one the possibility of radical perspective from which to see and create, to imagine alternatives, new worlds. (149–50)

Sekile's testimony reveals how she imagines possibilities both individually and collectively. And this feels like freedom, even if it is on the margin. I love how she is sharing her alternatives.

And sometimes I was with a partner, but that wasn't essential. And I think that was really important for me. To remember that this was my erotic, like independent of others. And it also helped me to remember . . . the young Sekile and how I used to like to flirt [*trails off*] on the dance floor. And so, because I kept saying, I don't know how to date women, I don't know how to figure out if women are into me. And these dating apps! All this just feels so overwhelming. But then, when I was there, I could tell when I looked, I could see if a person wanted to dance with me or if I felt brave to ask somebody to dance. And because that made sense to me, asking someone to dance, you know, and it felt [organic].

The wholeness of connecting with another, we see this time and time again in Sekile's testimony. Through her connecting with others, as lover or simply as friend or advocate, we can glimpse into a type of healing, spiritual healing, that Sekile engages. This is the type of healing that Shange (1997) describes in her choreopoem, where Black women come into their interior to find themselves. Through her spiritual healing, Sekile comes deeper into self-trust—her erotic. Lorde (1984, 54) reminds us that "the erotic is a measure between the beginning of our sense of self and the chaos of our strongest feelings." *And when we come into the erotic, our friendships, sexual and/or platonic, serve to resist male-dominated, heteronormative, racial, and patriarchal systems that often require conformity. Yes, the red I see when I engage in Sekile's testimony shows us that there is a more radical way of being, with self, with others, with structures.*

Yeah, and then I could read their energy, because in the dancing you can, figure it out. There's a nonverbal way in which you're engaging with each other. I'm able to then tell from a very natural act of dancing whether this person might be someone I might be interested in getting to know more past that dance. Right? And so that was the light bulb moment, like, oh, you have to go out dancing more. You have to go out. Like leave the fucking apps alone, just go out and dance more. Put yourself back in the world and meet women that way. It felt more organic, and then COVID happened and ruined my life. Right?!

Sekile fully and sensually walks into the bosom of her interior. She finds her interior place through dance, activism, truth-telling, being sensual, seeking sexual pleasure, and being open—this is how she understands her erotic. If this does not embody living the erotic, then I do not know what living the erotic is. This is what I wrote after we concluded our conversation. Sekile leaves us with one testimony, a how-to prose poem, of how to be heard, how to be seen, how to hear yourself, and how to see yourself—to live from a place of truth. Audre Lorde (1980) says, "for us all, it is necessary to teach by living and speaking those truths which we believe and know beyond understanding. Because in this way alone we can survive, by taking part in a process of life that is creative and continuing, that is growth" (22).

Sekile is falling in love with her own vision. By choosing not to walk the lines she is expected to walk in and speak boldly of her choices, she is, in fact, a wild Black woman. And as such, she and the other women who testify on these pages offer us a blueprint of living the erotic—truth-telling in all of its complexities.

Chapter 5

A Barefoot Girl Howling at the Moon

Val's Testimony

Prelude V

My daughter first introduced me to Val. She was in fourth grade and came home bubbling with excitement. Our conversation went something like this.

"Mom, this lady came to school today to tell stories. She was amazing."

"Tell me about the story? What was it about?" I replied.

Most of her responses and conversation were about Val and what a fantastic storyteller she is. Years later, when she was in high school, she burst into the house after school, declaring, "Guess who was at school today!" This time she remembered her name. In fourth grade, she remembered how Val made her feel and not her name. In high school, she remembered how "Ms. Val" made her feel, her name, and the story. She is now in college, and I'm sharing with her that I'm interviewing Ms. Val for this book project. She declares, "The Story Lady! I can still remember her from fourth grade. She's amazing. I love how she tells stories."

A Black woman storyteller came into my daughter's majority white school and held the girls in the palm of her hands as she shared her stories with my then fourth-grade daughter. My daughter cannot necessarily remember, in totality, what Val, or "Ms. Val," as she calls her, said, but she remembers how Val made her feel. And that is the essence of Valerie, Val. She is an amazing storyteller. During COVID-19, she offered story-time on Fridays via Facebook Live. And I was right there roaring along when she said, "OK, let me hear you roar," and intently listening to her tell stories. Valerie is an experience—a whole-body experience. And so, I am not surprised that my daughter has held on to that fourth-grade memory of Val's story time.

~

Val is a Black, Shaman storyteller who seems to cross boundaries and enter spaces seamlessly. Her laugh is effervescent and inviting, like the stories she shares. Through the energy she brings to her storytelling, one feels transported, the magic of the story becomes alive and tangible in ways that logic cannot easily explain.

Simplicity, soothing, fire, and grace are the words that come to mind as I sat and allowed the ancestors to guide me to receive Val's testimony. Val reminds me of a sunset, of a gentle breeze, and of the sound of rain on the tin roofs of the "back in the day" homes one would find in villages in Barbados. The spirit of Oshun helps to guide my write-up of Val. If you could see the recording of our testimonial session, you would better understand why the ancestors offered this guide for engaging with Val's testimony—when she speaks it as if you can see the words—the images become alive and vivid. The flatness of words on paper, the one-dimensional aspect, does not do a service to all that Val offers. I will try to do my best to make Val come alive in the way she did during our conversation.

But first, about the elements that serve as my portal into Val's testimony. It is worth noting that much of my engagement with Val's testimony is also shaped by my engagement with some of Alice Walker's writings and by the writings of Ntozake Shange—particularly how they engage nature. This is not to suggest that they are elements of analysis, as analysis is not what I am attempting to do. Instead, I use some of their writings to help explain my performative embodied reading of Val's testimony. I start with the sound of the rain and water in general.

I am cognizant of how water, particularly rain and its sound, and the waters of Oshun—the rivers—serve as the medium for engaging with Val's testimony. As I write in "Water's Memory/Memory of Water" (unpublished), "Water, then allows Black women to come back to their true selves—allowing the interior to be reflected on the exterior." The sound of the rain on the tin roofs invited me to enter a sovereign psychic space. And it did so not only through sound but also through touch or, more importantly, how I imagine the tactile feel of rain. When I feel the rain,

I can feel a softness similar to the lamb's ear plant. This sense of touch is associated with soft rain, where the drops offer a rhythm that suggests rest. At times, rain feels like oil, slick and dense. This is the feeling I associate with an intense downpour that sounds serious and menacing. Rain symbolizes many things. It can represent, on the positive end, rebirth, the end of a drought, or an invitation for self-reflection. Rain can also be associated with fear, foreboding, and a sense of melancholy. Water in general, and the rain specifically, is recognized as performative, textual, and imaginative.

As a metaphor, rain has been used by authors such as Audre Lorde. In the poem "From the House of Yemanjá," Lorde says, "mother, I need your blackness now/ as the august earth needs rain." August, in some places, can be a very dry and sweltering month, often leaving the earth parched. In the US, it is sometimes referred to as the "dog days of summer." And so, Lorde is invoking Yemanjá (the Black mother she calls upon) in the way that some would make a call for rain—to provide relief, to address the "fire"/destruction, "absence," or what is lacking so that she may have life renewed. In this case, it is her Black womanness that she asks the rain to renew.

In *Meridian*, Alice Walker (1976, 219) writes, "There is water in the world for us brought by our friends though the rock of mother and god vanishes into sand and we, cast out alone to heal and re-create ourselves." Water can be both healing and destructive—a giver and a taker of life. In what instance water turns from one to the other remains a mystery. Water, indeed, can be transformational. If only metaphorically, water allows Black women an opportunity to "unlock the doors of memory and assert an identity that is both placed and placeless" (Richards 2009, 261). The malleable nature of water allows it to traverse space(s), physical and spiritual, over time. Given its nature, water can bend time and claim space.

Water can also offer a sense of belonging. This sense of belonging can be symbolic, spiritual, physical, political, and/or social. In writing on the uses of water, Pamela Mittlefehldt (2003, 139) asserts, "in turning to mystery, to magic, to the waters of our origin, we ultimately are returning to ourselves." According to Terry Tempest Williams (1995, 28), "We are water . . . We can always return to our place of origin." Furthermore, "we are water people," and as such water is more than metaphoric as "Our bodies, like the great round of ocean, are pulled and held by the moon. We are creatures that belong here" (Hogan 1995, 108). As O. B. Lawuyi (1998) states, "Only rivers and seas are different. They are characterised by motion, and, hence they are not just sources of healing. They have been raised into 'deities' and are endowed with special powers. They are also suitable habitats for witches and ancestor spirits" (186).

Enter the Orisha Oshun. Oshun is a Yoruba water goddess often associated with female sensuality, love, and fertility. She is often depicted wearing yellow and surrounded by freshwater. Yellow is thought of as embodying warmth, joy, and energy. According to Robert Farris Thompson (2001, 261), Oshun "cures without fee, she gives the honeyed water to the child." Oshun is often associated with water (freshwater such as rivers) and mirrors. Mirrors are more than simply a tool for vanity. They also reflect Oshun's powers to help individuals "see" themselves in a way that allows them to construct/reconstruct their self-image—to become healthy (see Hale 2001, 214). Finally, Oshun is viewed as having a warrior spirit as she is known to fight on behalf of herself and her children. In Osgobo, Nigeria, a yearly practice for those devoted to Oshun and others of the Yoruba religion involves paying homage to her. They make a pilgrimage to the Oshun River, where they engage in sacrifice and make pleas for good health, for example. Thousands gather to cleanse themselves in the river and appeal to Oshun. Val's honeyed water lies in her storytelling. As a Shaman, Valerie helps us see ourselves, and in seeing ourselves, we are offered a space to heal. In my write-up of my testimony with Val, I often just allow her words to stand, offering a glimpse, ever so often, into how it brings me deeper into my interior, my honey water, as I don't want to impede your interaction with Val's testimony.

Now let's enter the sound and texture of Val's testimony.

Bare Breasts and Women Running: Wild

Aw, I love the way you tell a story. Tell me what comes to mind when you hear the word wild. By the time we get to the word wild, Val and I had talked for about thirty minutes.

Well, the image that comes to mind is just like wide-open chest and nothing held back. I see bare breasts. I see women running. I see the beach. I hear howling at the moon.

Dancing with your full self unabashedly loud.

Rolling in the grass.

I'm drawn in by the lyric of Val's talk on "wild." "Dancing with your full self unabashedly loud" *draws me in. Body, voice, and the erotic. This is what Val appears to be invoking here, this moment when the body and the voice comes together and are freely expressed. Thus, she is evoking a notion of the erotic that Lorde speaks about.*

From there, I write "sensuous," one of the three elements that constitute the erotic as understood by Audre Lorde. My scribbled notes also include "look at Sassafrass—Indigo has the 'moon in her mouth.'" Ntozake Shange (1982), in Sassafrass, Cypress & Indigo, *writes*

> Where there is a woman, there is magic. If there is a moon falling from her mouth, she is a woman who knows her magic, who can share or not share her powers. A woman with a moon falling from her mouth, roses between her legs, and tiaras of Spanish moss, this woman is a consort of the spirits. (27)

Indigo, a character in Sassafrass, Cypress & Indigo, *is known for having access to the moon, and this is partly because Indigo had to create her own world as* "there wasn't enough for Indigo in the world she'd been born to." *So, what did Indigo do? Like other Black women that Toni Morrison, for example, writes about, Indigo made up* "what she thought black people needed. Access to the moon. The power to heal. Daily visits with the spirits" (Shange 1982, 4–5). *Indigo embodies resistance and self-knowledge. She characterizes a feminine model of a wild woman/child. Val, like Indigo, through ritual and imagination, offers themself access to being healthy and whole in a context of race-gender domination. They imagine Black girlhood/womanhood outside of boundaries.*

Also scribbled in the margin is "without clothes." But I'm not talking about being without physical clothes. In my mind, I am thinking of being free of all the things we hide behind, those things that "cover us," and what it feels to be free of all that cloaks us. This is, in part, the sensuality that Lorde speaks of. Nikki Young (2012, 301) writes, "I employ Lorde's description of sensuality as an epistemological source in order to destabilize the polarization of mind and body. This destabilization is not only helpful in supporting a psychosomatic frame of knowing; it also encourages a new type of truth seeking that opens imaginative possibilities."

I find myself fascinated with how Val blurs the line between self/nature and mind/body. She suggests that such dualities are limiting as she engages with the cycles of life (loves the moon), thereby becoming one with cosmic energy. By speaking of being naked and bare chest howling at the moon, metaphorically and physically, Val is expressing freedom. Alice Walker in The Color Purple *(1982, 196) writes, "My first step away from the old white man was trees. Then air. Then birds. Then other people." Here, Walker articulates the significance of nature in her quest for freedom, allowing herself to be reborn so that she could be in community with others. Nature becomes a place of healing and restoration, a place that will enable one to enter into the interior.*

In the beginning of In Search of Our Mothers' Gardens, *Alice Walker (1983) details the tenets of womanism. Included on the list is a woman who* "Loves music. Loves dance. Loves the moon. Loves the Spirit. Loves love and food and roundness. Loves struggle. Loves the Folk. Loves herself. Regardless" *(xi–xii). Val's use of nature and how she imagines being in relation to nature speaks to this practice of love, which draws us deeper into our uses of the erotic. For example, we see Val's relationship with spirit and its connection to creativity (loves music and dance). In speaking on creativity, Audre Lorde tells us that when we operate from our erotic, our interior, it brings us to joy, creative joy. And such creative joy can be expressed by* "dancing, building a bookcase, writing a poem, examining an idea" *(1984, 57). Joy and sharing it by being in community may be* "physical, emotional, psychic," *or intellectual (1984, 56). Dancing, other creative endeavors, and luxuriating in nature are all a part of our creative empowerment. It can bring us deeper into self and our feelings, affording us an opportunity for renewal and spiritual renewal.*

When I think of my youngest freest self, which tends to be before ten, I think it is pretty typical for girls. For, you know, a lot of reasons it's prepubescent and in many ways, but also like in terms for me. We moved when I was ten and, you know, you are starting middle [*school*]—all these changes. But when I think about it now, I'm like, my God, did our parents know where we were because I felt so free. I felt so under the guise of adults doing this. Right. Well, actually, it's interesting because when my dad's mom lived in DC, she was called the "Axe" for battle axe. We did not call her that. Her three sons called her that. We called her grandma. You know, but Grandma raised three boys, and she did not know what to do with me. I was the only girl in the family. And we didn't spend a lot of time with her. But I would say she was the one who most tried to contain me. And that's interesting, right, because my mother's white. And so, it was my Black grandmother who was the one really trying to like rein me in. Now, of course, I think she knew some things about the world for Black women, you know that certainly, my mom didn't really know. But, other than yeah, so, the "Axe" was always trying to rein me in [*laughter*]. But for the most part, I was a very wild child. I was barefoot.

In her biomythography, Zami: A New Spelling of My Name, *Lorde opens with a story of her mother. It is worth noting that Lorde's mother, Linda, immigrated from the Caribbean and settled in Harlem, New York. Audre places her understanding of her identity, racial and sexual, in the context of her experiences with her mother. There are moments of tenderness and reprimand, and it is in this duality that I imagine Val's experiences with "Axe." An experience where lines are drawn as a means of protection, an understanding of protection that grows from these matrilineal figures' experiences with their intersecting identities, but lines, nevertheless.*

Well, some of the change that I started to say was that my family moved from one neighborhood to another right before I skipped fourth grade, and I ended up going into fifth grade, which was the beginning of my starting to feel less than. Because even though I was old [relative to those in fourth grade], which is part of [*trails off*], you know, they didn't have talented programs back then. So, they sometimes [*skipped us*], and I was early in the year. You know, and I was taller than everybody, so they decided I was going to skip fourth grade. She's going to go into fifth grade, and those girls were just enough older—older than me—for me to start to feel a little bit insecure. Not only that, you know, and their bodies were doing things that mine wasn't quite yet. And then by the time I got to [*trails off*]. So, I started to feel a little bit insecure there.

And then I also had an interracial friendship, which had a big challenge with her father kind of all at the same time. So, all of a sudden, there's this racial component that I wasn't very, you know, hadn't mattered up until that time. And then Carlene and I became friends, and then she wasn't allowed to be friends with me because I was a Black kid. We spent a whole undercover week together when her parents went away on vacation, and then she told her parents and then that was like, boom! So that caused a shut down for me. You know, I have a whole story that I sometimes tell. But like I, [*trails off*] it was one of those things where I didn't talk about it fully with my parents, like they kind of knew, but they didn't because I was coming up to that age where you don't tell your parents everything either. Like I had to ask permission to go and play over there with Carlene, and they were like, "Really?" And then, when it all went sideways, they also didn't ask a lot of questions. And I stuffed it . . . and I mean like buried it.

Lines, racial lines, lines drawn around our bodies, and our knowledge. Friendships ending because of race and how Val speaks to burying her feelings show us how lines limit our possibilities to live our erotic. Like the character Indigo, there wasn't always space for Val.

Um, and then there was still a wildish part of me, right; like in high school, I was never the cool kid, and I wasn't the wild, rebellious kid who wanted to drink and do drugs. Oh, I didn't have any interest in that, really. Mostly because I was still thinking I wanted to travel the world. You know, I just had these things that I wanted to do. So, I can remember in high school, we were sort of, my crowd was kind of nerdy. You know because we wanted to have like theme parties. You know what I mean? We weren't really interested in getting drunk and smoking pot or whatever. But we would have these costume—elaborate costume parties and do these progressive dinner things and stuff. The wild part was really the nonconforming. In terms of nonconforming, what it meant to be cool because it wasn't cool, but also nonconforming to what it meant to be, you know, the druggie type people. So, in our day, "back in our day" [*she chuckles with mirth*] we call them rags.

So, you had like the cool people over here and the stoners over here. I was [*trails off*]. We were in the band. We called ourselves the loser club for a while like we just called ourselves "The Losers" because we were the band geeks. You know. But I did the band, and I did the chorus. I did all the artsy things that I could possibly do and loved that. And then when I got to college, at Brown [*University*], finding storytelling and just again, sort of . . . I guess it's sort of bold, but . . . But it just was so normal in a way to me that I didn't really . . . I guess it's kind of rolling downhill, but it's not really being all that big about it, you know if that makes sense.

Yeah, yeah. It's like, no, I'm just gonna do this. I walked into Rites and Reasons Theatre. And I was like, oh my god, I found home and, to be with George [*Huston Bass*] and to be with, you know Black artists who were telling stories from Black perspectives, and I had no interest in the white theater department for a long time. I was really nurtured at Rites and Reason Theatre, and again with that George connection and the Langston Hughes connection and that sense of like live your life, tell your story. Don't try to fit into other people's notion of who it is you're here on this planet to be. So, I would say that certainly continued. And even now, you know it. I'm fifty-four years old, and I'm trying to adopt a two-year-old; that's fucking crazy. But hey! Because I've never done it in the right or, you know, I've never done anything in the order that you're supposed to but just when the time is right.

As I listen to Val speak of how she was able to find home, I'm reminded of the healing nature of Oshun, a nurturer of humanity, and how so many go to her waters in search of healing. The theater is Val's version of healing waters. For many who engage in the text "Uses of the Erotic," community is often overlooked as a place of interrogation, of living the erotic. Yet Lorde tells us that "the erotic functions for me in several ways and the first is in providing the power which comes from sharing deeply any pursuit with another person" (1984, 56). *Lorde speaks of how the erotic is experienced in community and the joy it offers. She implies that the joy of engaging the erotic in community results, not necessarily, from taking but from sharing and honoring differences that may exist. This sharing gives way to the communal experience of joy as it does not rest in a patriarchal and capitalist notion of competition. And this is what I believe Val experienced when she walked into the Rites and Reasons Theatre. And no, I am not suggesting that all who engaged in this space operate outside of patriarchy and capitalism. Instead, I'm suggesting that Val could find a community within this space that allowed her to access her erotic and do so in community.*

If You're Lucky, You Can Enter the Interior

Now for the word interior.

First word was dark.
Juicy
Private
Mysterious
If you're lucky, you can enter

Well, I say if you're lucky, you can enter because of the privacy and because it is where the treasures live. Right?! And it is to be explored and also protected.

I find myself moaning as Val testifies. Eventually, I find the words: "I love how you frame it—it's where the treasures lie." I ask, "What kind of treasures?"

I'm just going with images. So that's where the heart is. Right. The real. The heart, meaning the place of love. The vulnerable spot. Which is the part that God knows and [*trails off*]. And maybe it feels like it's the place that only God knows, right!?

There is something about how Val inserts this thought in her testimony that captures my attention. Was she asking me if the erotic is only known by

God? If so, how or when does God allow us to see the interior? I've lingered on this for some time and cannot pretend to have an answer.

I like how Val says that the interior is to be simultaneously explored and protected. It is some place of value she seems to suggest, yet it is not off-limits to those willing to venture in. Maybe that is why Lorde said that the erotic is so feared. When the erotic is explored and treasured, treated as something of great value, it moves into the transformative realm. And those who control many of society's resources would prefer that the masses not engage in this transformative process because our work would take on a different quality, as suggested by Audre Lorde.

Um, I think I can get to know it, I would say, spiritual [*trails off*]. The getting to know it is part of the spiritual practice, right, or the prayer time or the singing time or the writing time or the holding the baby while she sleeps time that tears open a little part of the heart, or softens the edges. But the thing about the interior is that work is required to get there. Well, if you go to the Grand Canyon, you can stand on the edge and look out upon the vista, which is stunning. But if you want to go into the Grand Canyon, you have to prepare. And you have to have . . . I don't know. How many days to actually make the journey?

Um, and that's the way it is for your, for my, interior, right? Like it's the Shamanic training has been those places in particular where there's plenty of time and safe space to enter deeply into there. You don't just chill. And sometimes you need a guide. And sometimes you need like to leave that red thread so you can find your way back out. Bread crumbs won't do it because somebody might gobble them up on the way. Right, so holy moonlight. Girl, it is divine teaching joy to howl at the moon at the edge of the sea. It is that sense of what is truly sacred. It's hard to say.

And I guess that's the part of it that the divinity or the *divine* is what Brother Blue, who was this amazing storyteller, used to say that it's like where the breath of life fills you right where you're breathing in the breath of life. The beginning of the beginning and that is when you know that you are truly a part of all that is divine. If I think [more about divine] the other word that's coming is like the two phases, right, like divine knowing. It's like you just know it all in your being and all around you, and you know it's not you. So, the divine is you and not you, and you and not you together.

I keep coming back to rain and how I imagine it sliding between my fingers. In this case, I imagine that it feels smooth and just a tad slippery—

like velvet, black velvet. As it is soothing, it invites me/you in. In essence, I/ you am/are invited to come in and get to know myself/ yourself a bit better, to sit and explore. Maybe the image of the baby sleeping in your lap evokes this reflection on rain. Like a raindrop that slowly slides down the windowpane, I linger on "the beginning of the beginning" *and how that allows us to come to know ourselves, our divine selves. This is the place of power that Audre Lorde summons us to get to know. Val proposes that this is the place when we truly connect with our erotic and begin to live. In a similar vein, Audre Lorde writes that the erotic is the* "lifeforce of women" *(1984, 55). She and Val are both exploring the capacity for self-connection and self-awareness. But this is not about self-connection and awareness for individual gain only, as it leads to a place of freedom that is simultaneously individual and collective.*

In thinking of the nature of our (self) awareness, Lorde offers honey water that allows us to speak to disembodiment through the confrontation of domination and control and show how we can resist via truth-telling and creating a world we imagine—as Indigo did. This brings me to ways of knowing, Black women's ways of knowing. As a little girl, I remember my gran would say, "Sometimes I have ways of knowing." *These ways of knowing are not easily quantifiable or may seem to defy logic, as expected by Western philosophic thought. Still, they are valid ways of knowing self and society. Audre Lorde (1980, 65) speaks about ways of knowing when she wrote,* "In order to keep me available to myself, and be able to concentrate my energies upon the challenges of those worlds through which I move, I must consider what my body means to me." *Considering what one's body means to self represents a type of literacy that Black women invoke in their quest for self-articulation. LeConté Dill and colleagues (2019, 74) write that Black girls formulate an understanding of self and community by* "drawing upon their internal resources as they subsist and conceive of their own future identities, opportunities, and experiences." *And to do this, they come into their bodies; they become available to self. This availability to self allows them to tap into their feelings that are then used to be in community. In essence, Black girls and women rely on their ways of knowing, listening to their bodies, as Lorde speaks of in her telling of her experiences with breast cancer. And they use the knowledge offered to them via their bodies to determine what is good for them and their communities. This is what Val means when she says,* "It's like you just know it all in your being."

Flowing Is How I Imagine Feminine

Let's talk about feminine.

I'm just going to go with all the words that just flew through my mind. So, a sense of flowing,

Flow
Soft and hard
Wild and free
Meant to be served
Deep with feeling
A mother's lap
A weeping willow
The hands that prepare the meal
And hold the baby and,
Dying elders

The feminine shows up when needed and can sit quietly.

"See, now I don't even want to mess with any of that. It is just so perfectly beautiful." This was my response as we recorded the interview and even upon review. I still want this just to sit and be.

No. Well, the moon. The waves on the sand, the cycles of life, reminding us that this too shall pass. And this too shall pass! And that life does not ever end I feel is feminine.

And I moaned! Cycles of life . . . does not ever end.

See getting out of the way, just letting it come on through.

And again, I moan. This is a testimony I needed to hear.

That Heat: Energy

Energy is the next word

Lord, I wish I had me some [*lots of laughter*].

There is the effervescent laugh that opens the door and draws you in. Val's laughter is communal, is my thought. It invites you to come in, sit and just be. I guess that is what she means by the feminine, "it shows up when needed." *Her laugh seems to embody the feminine. And her laugh belies her claim of needing energy as it is filled with a kind of energy that is soothing, like the gentle pitter-patter of the rain on the roof. I imagine the healing powers of Oshun—the healing waters that so many seek to immerse themselves in in hopes that they come away whole.*

Oh, I know, listen, they tell me it's [*energy*] gonna come back. I crack up. My friend said the other day, "It gets better, you know, though it's really hard. But it gets better." I'm like, OK. Then I say motherhood and menopause are an interesting combination. Let me just say that. Because of the energy, right. Energy is the heat you feel with another person or in the right space. Like you can feel the vibration. It's the living vibration that exudes from every living thing. And it can be, and you know we're sensitive to it. Right? So, it can be a high energy, could be a low energy, it can be a positive energy, or it can be a real negative energy. So again, it kind of goes back to being sensitive to what you feel. Right? Because when we're tapping, you know that exercise that people do? Where you put your hands together, right, and then you pull them apart. And can you feel like [*energy*]. We all have that if we're paying attention to it. And you know, we have to be careful of our energy, because sometimes you give it. Give it, give it, and are getting nothing back. Really energy, it ought to be reciprocal, and when it is right, there's some sort of loop. So, it does become important to pay attention to that. Like, am I putting out a lot of energy, and what is coming back to me? Are there places and spaces that I need to conserve my energy, withdraw my energy? Yes. And as I say that I, you know, I'm not always good at that.

"I think as women, as Black women, sometimes we aren't as good because there's so much in the world that pulls on our energy."

Yeah.

"You know there is so much external to us that sucks our energy. Sometimes just waking up not knowing what lies ahead, and you know you turn on the news. You don't know what's gonna happen."

That's right. That's right. And so, one of the things that I appreciate about the Shamanic practice, and I think a bunch of indigenous practices, is that they, you know, they teach you to cloak yourself. So that you can preserve, not only preserve your energy but protect yourself from the assaults of that other energy that can just really wound us.

The thing that just popped in my head was the grounding in the earth. And how important that is.

As a, as a source to give energy to me or to us, right. It's real to stand on the earth, particularly barefoot. And it's also, you know, she's willing to take it. To release and to ground in her. To help maintain balance.

Audre Lorde (1984) says,

> My fullest concentration of energy is available to me only when I integrate all the parts of who I am, openly, allowing power from particular sources of my living to flow back and forth freely through all my different selves, without the restrictions of externally imposed definition. Only then can I bring myself and my energies as a whole to the service of those struggles which I embrace as part of my living. (120–121)

She and Val speak of this notion of flow, reciprocity with self and others, self and society. But how, as a Black woman, can we live in this flow? We have to be sensitive to what we feel, Val says. She says this helps us guard and protect our energies as Black women. Being sensitive to how we feel serves as a guide for analyzing the lines we are often expected to exist within. The lines often prevent us from being wild, fragmenting our energy so that it is not flowing from a place of truth—the "beginning of the beginning."

Lorde and Val suggest that to be in the flow requires one to be in tune with self—to know self. To know self is to look in the mirror, an invitation to the interior, that Oshun offers. Too often, the external world does not see Black women and can shape how Black women see themselves. As Lorde suggests, fear is an element used to limit how and if we can see ourselves. Further, Lorde suggests that by limiting the uses of the erotic, our self-actualization becomes stunted. Thus, to see oneself, and in truth, allows for self-actualization and an opportunity to live in the erotic and the possibility of being whole—which Osun offers by giving us a mirror. And this is what Val reminds us to do—to look in the mirror and see self fully.

An Opening Up to What Feels Good: The Erotic

Now for the erotic. What comes to mind?

The erotic. It's all senses for me like I'm like smeared with chocolate. I just want to lick [*it*]. The senses are when I pay attention to the senses. What does it feel like really paying attention to that? And what does it smell like? What does it taste like? Even sounds like, you know, what are those sounds that just slow the heart? An open[*ing*]. Erotic is an opening up to what feels good. Yeah, I mean, it feels like senses to me, like taking the time to really delight in touch. To savor. Lingering feels erotic. Closing your eyes so you can really taste. Or smell, you know. Like can you focus on one of those senses in a full way feels really erotic to me. And I think because I'm such a heady person as an Aquarius, you know that that's what it is telling me to [*do*]; get out of the head. To those senses to the body. The body. Of course, you know, the mind helps.

If the rain had a color, it would be yellow as it is filled with sensual energy. Rain can offer us a whole-body experience, the type of experience expressed by Val, which brings me back to Indigo, the wild child/woman. Through her visits with the spirits and her access to the moon, Indigo could heal (Shange 1982, 27) in a way similar to Oshun. They draw on the energy of the moon and water to heal. To heal the divide that happens when we are not living and using our erotic, we have to harness the energy, the golden honey, that allows us to go deep inside so that we can experience all of who we are to be able to feel, engage the sensuous so that we can come back into the world to effect change. Through her testimony, Val shows us how to feel and to feel fully. Therein lies the power of feeling that Audre Lorde discusses throughout her works.

Chapter 6

Since I Am Divine and I Am Feminine, It Is All Me

Lakeesha's Testimony

Prelude VI

Of the women who shared their testimonies, Lakeesha is the one woman whom I am least familiar with. On January 28, 2019, I was researching for another project, and I stumbled across "Healing through (Re) Membering and (Re)Claiming Ancestral Knowledge about Black Witch Magic" (Harris 2018). In that chapter, Lakeesha wrote, "I come from a long line of Black spirit women who first believed in freedom and then used everything in their power, including their magic, conjure, and other forms of African traditional religious and spirit work, in movement toward that freedom" (n.p.).

I was captivated by "I come from a long line of Black spirit women." To date, I do not fully understand why that particular line intrigued me. It is easy to say that I was captivated because it is beautifully composed. But maybe it is the power of naming that drew me in—it seems that Lakeesha named herself in a way that could not be dismissed. I had yet to conceptualize *Erotic Testimonies*, or maybe the idea of it was buried in my recess. Yet when the idea of this book germinated, in January 2020, I remembered reading Lakeesha's piece and immediately thought I must include Lakeesha Harris as one of the wild women to interview.

Lakeesha was the most challenging of the women for me to pin down and schedule some time to chat with. I reached out on Facebook through Black Witches University, asking if anyone knew how to contact her or if they would be willing to help me contact her. And as they say, it is a small world; Sekile is friends with Lakeesha—they share a passion for justice work, particularly reproductive justice work. With introductions made, I tried to schedule our time to chat. And that was a bit of a challenge. It was challenging because Lakeesha was busy making her dreams real with home ownership (which, as you will read, is connected to her sense of justice and liberation). She was doing it in the midst of what I call the power pandemics—COVID-19 and state-sanctioned violence against Black bodies, minds, and spirits. And in the middle of her expansion, she faced a series of hurricanes. It feels important to name her experience. It is as if a force says, tell them about this woman who is striving for justice and liberation amid power pandemics and storms. And then I wonder: maybe that is what makes Lakeesha wild.

Using her own words, I introduce Lakeesha Harris.

> Let's see. I am Lakeisha Juanita Harris, that is the name my mother gave me; that's the one I stick with even though I've been given many names, you know, through initiations, um, and African Spiritual traditions. I am the daughter of Yemaya. I am a Black Witch and Healer. And I hold that space for the women who will come, people who will come and think that they have lost their mind, and I'm thinking, "Oh! You've found the right place! You've come to the right place!" [*laughter*] (interview)

"You've come to the right place!" That is exactly how I felt when I stumbled across Lakeesha's writing. Lakeesha situates her healing work as political:

> I have always been a healer and caretaker—of *others*, whether through formal employment or informally in my community. I graduated high school with a diploma and a certification as a certified nursing assistant (CNA), and I did that work for many years. I later became a doula, a birthing assistant who helps the mother and entire family unit (if desired) from prenatal, all the way up to birth, and then after the baby comes home.

> I performed such duties as assisting mothers with lactation support and acclimation to motherhood. This is important political work because sometimes Black women are so disconnected from family, and family can be harmful depending on what the individual's situation is. Creating a non-judgmental, loving, healing space so that one can actualize their own definition of motherhood is empowering. (Harris 2018, n.p., emphasis in original)

Lakeesha Harris personifies what I imagine when I think of wild Black women. She engages in self-definition, self-actualization, healing, and justice work. She sees beyond herself, giving way to her engagement with the community—building and supporting in community (this is discussed in more detail in the concluding chapter). Lakeesha is a holder of sacred space. That's what I wrote upon the completion of her testimony. And it is in her holding of sacred space we can see how she invokes an Afrocentric and womanist cosmological spiritual system that speaks to healing and freedom.[1]

As I sat with the ancestors waiting for their guidance on engaging Lakeesha's testimony, I was shown the color green and Oya.[2] A review of color psychology suggests that green is a calming color, which may be because of its association with nature (see Cherry 2020). Green is also thought to invoke compassion and a sense of optimism (Cherry 2020). The spirits that Audre Lorde told me to allow to guide my interaction with the testimonies of these wild Black women are amazing. Consider that it was after I had jotted down the notes that were conjured, the knowledge of the ancestors, and after I read Lakesha's piece, I now realize that Lakeesha speaks of Oya in that chapter that I found so captivating. I do not even remember seeing this when I first read her chapter. Audre Lorde, speaking from her current space, knew precisely what she was doing. As it is with these wild Black women, my job is to simply listen and allow the ancestors' knowledge to pour forth. Their giving of Oya is also part of the testimony of how the ancestors speak.

Oya was offered to me to engage Lakeesha before she encountered the hurricanes that assaulted Louisiana. Oya, a Yoruba deity, is often associated with wind—calm and violent. Consequently, Oya can be a gentle breeze, a hurricane, or a tornado. In characterizing Oya, Judith Gleason (1987 1) says that she is "the leader of the market women in Yoruba communities . . . offers special protection and encouragement in negotiation with civil authorities and arbitration disputes. Thus, one may speak of Oya as patron of feminine leadership, of persuasive charm reinforced by àjé—an efficacious gift usually translated as 'witchcraft.'" As you engage in your own performative embodied reading of Lakeesha's testimony, I hope that you can understand why Oya and the color green were given for her.

Wild: Give Me the Crazy People

Let's chat about the word wild.

Crazy.

"Okay, tell me more," I said as we chatted. I admit I was shocked and intrigued by this response and couldn't wait to have Lakeesha elaborate.

So, like I was saying with "you've lost your mind." I don't feel like crazy is a bad term. I feel, you know, whatever is not in alignment with what people see outside of what you're supposed to do or mainstream culture or the way in which you hold on to these very hegemonic ideas about how you're supposed to be, you're going to be labeled as crazy. You're going to be labeled as eccentric. You're going to be labeled as somebody that is outside of the context of what normal is, right?

And oftentimes, people will be like, "She's crazy!" I'm not crazy! I feel like I'm the sanest person in the room. What are you talking about?

But I feel people will always be like, you know, "she crazy" as a bad word. And I feel like for me, give me the crazy people; I'll take them. Because they push us to think about greater needs in society, like right now, people, the crazy people, are pushing us towards liberation, towards mental health, addressing the needs of people who have mental health issues. And that's not crazy. They need help.

My attempts to engage this testimony also found me reading and rereading the short story "Blossom, Priestess of Oya, Goddess of Winds, Storms and Waterfalls" *in Dionne Brand's ([1988] 1989)* Sans Souci and Other Stories. *Blossom immigrated from Trinidad to Canada, married an abusive man, and worked a series of dead-end jobs. Given the totality of her experiences, Blossom has a moment where she seemingly breaks down—she is crying and screaming in the street.*

> Next thing Blossom know, she running Victor down Vaughan Road screaming and waving the bread knife. She hear somebody screaming loud, loud. At first, she didn't know who it is, and is then she realize that the scream was coming from she and she couldn't stop it. She dress in she nightie alone and screaming in the middle of the road. . . . She wake up the next morning, feeling shaky and something like spiritual. She was frightened, in case the crying come back again. . . . She had the feeling that she was holding she body around she heart, holding sheself together, tight, tight. She get dressed and went to the Pentecostal Church where she get married and sit there till evening. For two weeks this is all Blossom do. . . . During these weeks she could drink nothing but water. (38)

Some interpret Blossom's behavior as a mental breakdown. However, I read this as Blossom's journey into the interior—her interior. Given all the oppression Blossom faced—race-gender-class oppression, she resisted the anti-Blackness and behaviors grounded in patriarchy. And like Lakeesha, she went to the interior, embracing what may on the surface appear as one thing but is indeed a response to violence and an attempt to name this violence.

Lakeesha's claim of crazy stems from her desire to resist silencing mechanisms and the often-resulting erasure. We see this in her claim "So, they allow us to see all of the parts of society that are missing that need to be addressed." *Blossom and Lakeesha engage in a politics of recognition. Both reject some societal norms, considering that crazy is stigmatized, to critique society and (re)invent themselves. Blossom's and Lakeesha's empowerment is not birthed through social and/or political institutions. Instead, it comes from them both going deep into the interior and spending time there recognizing and listening, deeply, to their truths. Thus, in fiction and real life, we witness Black women's politics of recognition.*

And, you know, there was a time where my Black queer self would have been labeled crazy just because—or put in an institution because of who I am, right?

I'm not crazy. I feel like I'm being pushed more towards the liberatory self, my freedom. Every day I'm being pushed towards my freedom and challenged in ways to get that freedom. And they may [*call*] me crazy, but I'm OK with that term.

"So, tell me a little bit about this notion. You mentioned this a couple of times, this notion of the liberatory self. What does that mean to you? What is that?"

But there was a time when I was in graduate school, and I was just like I'm either going to get free, or I'm going to take my own life. And I had to go off to investigate what that freedom looked like at the time, and for a mother who had been raising six kids, working two and three jobs. You know, also going through school while doing it, undergrad, and then on to grad school, I felt suffocated within the ivory tower. I felt suffocated in my role as a mother. I had all of these roles and responsibilities and no breathing room.

So, at that moment, my liberatory self looked like giving myself a little breathing room, and I looked to my partner and said, "Look. This is what it is; I either go off or kill myself, and then you don't have me at all." So, I went off for a year, and that's when I came down to New Orleans for the first time.

Carole Boyce Davies ([1994] 1999, 17) notes, "Because [black women] were/are products of separations and dislocations and dis-memberings, people of African descent in the Americas historically have sought reconnection." *Space, physical and psychic space, allows Lakeesha to find herself to reconnect in the way that Boyce Davies describes. New Orleans was her version of Blossom's Pentecostal church, the place she would visit to manage the journey into her interior. Space allowed/allows Lakeesha to move beyond prescribed ways of being that can be limiting and rigid at times. In* Zami: A New Spelling of My Name (1982, 177*), we see how Audre Lorde uses space to simultaneously recognize and resist constraining limits. This is particularly evident in her use of* "sister-outsiders." Sister Outsider *was used to speak to Lorde's experiences as a Black gay woman living in New York City during the 1950s. The naming of her experience, her truth, allows Lorde to tap into her erotic, thereby allowing her to pry open a space for Black women's self-identification.*

Lorde often writes of herself as a "Black lesbian feminist warrior poet mother." And in this conceptualization, Lorde engages in a critique of hegemonic categories that can limit the naming herself—the lines I discuss in chapter 1. Lorde (1984) writes:

> As a forty-nine-year-old Black lesbian feminist socialist mother of two, including one boy, and a member of an interracial

> couple, I usually find myself a part of some group defined as other, deviant, inferior, or just plain wrong. . . . I find I am constantly being encouraged to pluck out some one aspect of myself and present this as the meaningful whole, eclipsing or denying the other parts of self. But this is a destructive and fragmenting way to live. (114, 120)

Power! To name self is to assert power. And Audre Lorde recognizes the value of such power when she said that a failure to name oneself means that "there is no contact with personal power; without that contact of power there is no movement; and without there's surely death." *(Hammond 1980, 19). Lakeesha exercises this power when she names herself and her desires. In doing such, she is circumventing death in all of its forms—physical, spiritual, psychological, and political.*

And it was the first time that I had a room of my own where I can just wake up and not hear the noise of, you know, children just being children. And there was nothing wrong with my children; they were just being children. It was something wrong with me because I needed breath. I needed to breathe. And so, the liberatory self felt [*that*] for [*the*] liberatory me that needed to be, [*I*] needed room to breathe. [*Liberatory me*] needed to hear her own voice. Outside of the context of mother, and student, and partner.

I needed to start to define who I was and just think, light a candle for myself, just pee and not have nobody open the bathroom door, you know!

These basic things that I feel like maybe people with privilege would take for granted, somebody who had maybe had a nanny. But I was writing my undergraduate thesis while frying bacon and doing all the other things. I had no way to just be, just be me.

"To define who I was." *This is the power I felt when I first encountered Lakeesha via her writing. This is the power of Oya—leading women to self-sufficiency, their liberatory self. To define self is a liberatory practice; as Lorde says, not doing so would mean consumption by those who engage in the act of definition.*

So, my liberatory self was being defined then. And so, my liberatory [*trails off*]. I say that to say there is a point where we have to reassess what liberation looks like for us in the context of the moment.

What does liberation look like? I have been pondering this question for some time now. Asking myself what liberation, that decenters whiteness, looks like for me as a Black woman? I write:

Allowing/permission,[3]
Open/centered,
Freedom/curiosity,
Love/warmth.
Self/whole.
Spaces of rest.

Right now, my liberatory self looks like owning my home and land and being free of like putting my money into someone else's land or a rental for generations. I'm the first in my family, since slavery, to actually purchase a home. My grandmother couldn't do it. My great-grandmother didn't do it. My mother couldn't do it.

Oya is known for bringing self-sufficiency, especially to women. Blossom, the protagonist of Brand's short story, is visited by the Goddess Oya. Through Oya, she can pursue a successful entrepreneurial career—and claim ownership of herself. But this is not a simple story of individual transformation. Indeed, it is a story of how African-descended people resist oppression—oppression from slavery, colonialism, and neocolonialism—as Blossom's individual experiences with oppression also represent oppression faced by African-descended peoples. And this is what I hear when I listen to Lakeesha speak of ownership—this is more than just material ownership of land and property (which are essential), but this is also about "warring against her own history of suffering" *(Mullins 2012, 13).*

So, for me, that was liberation, to be able to not just own a house, though, right? A house where I, I, feel like I couldn't have conjured better on it because there's land for me to grow food. And gardening has saved my life, like constructing growth space and being one with the earth. So, it has stabilized me in a way that I have been able to teach my students, and it has stabilized them. So being able to have something of my own that I can pass down, that my great grandmother wasn't able to do, my grandmother, my mother was not able to do, looks like liberation for me.

In writing about literature, particularly in her analysis of Black women's literature, Saskia Fürst (2017, 68) *says,* "At the same time, the female characters' life stories—their very bodies and identity developments—exist as palimpsests of the oral stories, cultural practices, and African cosmologies of the ancestral women whose lives are being remembered, (re)written and, therefore, revised." *Lakeesha takes this theorization and shows us how it manifests in the real lived experiences of Black women. She defines what liberation looks like not just for her but also for her past and future lineage.*

And what is beautiful is how she imagines stability as a communal practice achieved through self-definition, which is in part achieved through conjuring.

A Place of Magic: The Interior

Interior. What comes to mind?

Oh! [*deep sigh*]

Henrietta Lacks.

When I think of interior, I think of the magical Black woman and our ability to, really heal not just us, but a whole freakin' world. And Henrietta's very tangible contribution to that healing from inside of her body was her cervix cells that has fed cancer research, and polio vaccines, and so much.

And when I say Black Girl Magic, I really am talking about the physical application of magic and our ability to create something out of nothing. And so, you think about Henrietta and her cells, her interior, literally, her cervix cells, and the application of her magic to be able to, to be the only cells on the planet that can re-create, re-create and feed generations and generations of curing power.

Black
Girl
Magic

Black Girl Magic is a celebrated and, at times, contested term. Yet, Black women have, through history, deployed the term "magic" to position themselves both in relation to power and outside of power structures (see Jordan-Zachery and Harris 2019; Walker 1983). In the introduction to Black Girl Magic Beyond the Hashtag, *my co-editor Duchess Harris and I argue that there are four, at least, elements associated with #BlackGirlMagic:* "Community building and making, as Black Girl Magic serves as a form of intra-communication methodology; challenging dehumanizing representations via a practice of self-definition; rendering Black femmes, girls and women visible, and restoring what is sometimes violently taken" *(Jordan-Zachery and Harris 2019, 14–24). This is what Lakeesha is referencing when she speaks of Black girl magic. AND she is speaking to the conjuring power of Black women. We see her do this work via Black Witch University. In an interview about Black Witch University, Lakeesha says,* "Black Witch

University is defined as Audre Lorde says, 'The master's tools will never dismantle the master's house.' So, what will dismantle the master's house? Your tools. Go and reclaim your tools. Your magic will dismantle the master's house" (Ramgopal, 2016). *Black Witch University is understood as* "a maroon mystery school and scared spiritual space for Black witches of the Diaspora," *according to their Facebook page.*

So, when I think about interior, I think about what in me do I have to contribute for generations and generations and generations to come? And we do it all the time. I feel, as Black women, we are the healers and the givers [*trails off*], our breast milk. Our just everything, every facet of our body is indeed magic.

"So how do you curate your interior? What do you do?"

Oh! So, I have been doing really well lately, so I have been making sure that I am juicing. One of my best friends, who died recently, I believe she died from COVID because she had some underlying issues. But her family hasn't talked about it. But they did cremate her body, according to COVID protocols. But the last gift she gave me was a housewarming gift of a juicer. She asked me, what do you want? I was like, well, I haven't been able to juice, my last juicer conked out on me. And so, she sent me that. And so, I had been juicing.

But even before that, I have been doing mutual aid. So, I have been creating tinctures for community members to keep them healthy during COVID. Tinctures in which I've taken myself. I have quarantined to make sure that I'm healthy. I am at this point, [*of making*] sure that I limited my interaction with people. And that is to say that, you know, it is a priority that we start to prioritize our own health and self.

Black women, mutual aid, friendships, and care. In Zami, *Audre Lorde centers the mythical and real-life nurturing aspects of female bonding through her stories of the Carriacou women or Zami. Zami is a testimony of Lorde's faith in and commitment to sisterhood and coalition-building among women. Through her various writings and speeches, Lorde espouses her view of sisterhood and relationships, sexual and nonsexual, between women, as a means of resisting systematic oppression. Like Lorde, Lakeesha offers us a cultural (de)construction and Black feminist imagination of the Black female self and body, thereby advancing a Black feminist agenda that not only repudiates epistemic race-gender violence but that shows us a way of building a society that is grounded in recognition of differences and mutual aid. To borrow from Analouise Keating's (2000) description of June Jordan's work, Lakeesha engages an* "interactional identity." *This means that she connects self/individual improvement and* "self-naming" *to the larger community's progress, thus blurring the lines between me/them or I/we.*

And so, I walk in the morning. I used to do marathons and triathlons, and now walking feels good to me. I would love to start back doing triathlons and marathons. And for now, I just enjoy walking along the levee, and I love being with water. So yeah, dumping myself in saltwater, taking ritual and spiritual baths, because not just about physical healing, it is about the ceremony of giving yourself a bath and cleansing the negative energy off and day-to-day rituals and offering to my spirit guides and Orisha, my warriors protecting my house and land space. So those are a few things that I've done to make sure that my inside is kept.

In Sister Outsider, *Audre Lorde speaks about* "the yes within ourselves" *(1984, 57). In Brand's short story, we are offered a literary understanding of what it means to find and live the "yes within ourselves." And Lakeesha offers an embodied testimony of what living that yes, found on the interior, looks like and how it is manifest. Across these three women, real and imagined, we are offered testimonies of bodily self-autonomy.*

Through life narratives, poems, and so on, Lorde reinterprets her body, providing insight into what it means to live with illness, cancer, and pain caused by societal race-gender practices that result in oppression. We get to see how Lorde experiences pain while expressing that women, regardless of social location, have the power and authority of self-governance. When Blossom taps into the power of Oya, she expresses a similar sentiment of self-governance and body autonomy. Through "magic," these women show how they enter into a space that counters disembodiment, bringing together the mind, body, and spirit within a community of women. And this is a use of the erotic. Lakeesha actively works to keep her insides, her interior, by doing "body work," which includes tending to the physical, the spiritual (ritual baths and honoring the Orishas), the political (using land to heal), and the communal (making tinctures). This is ultimately an exercise in self-actualization and truth living that seeks to counter the disembodiment faced by many Black women.

Divine: The Presence of Me and You Is Divine

Divine

Me.

I feel like people think divine exists outside of them, and it just does not. The presence of me and you is divine. Two black women conversing about what divine is divine. But also, spirit don't exist outside of us. I don't care what you believe in, whatever you call it. If it's God, it exists within you; everything in this universe exists in the context of women, people in general. So, I see myself as part of the divine. When I look at you, I see you as part of the divine and everybody else.

"I absolutely love it. I just wish most people would look a little inside themselves to find what they're so outwardly looking for. But we'll get there. We'll get there." I offer this, in the moment, in response to Lakeesha's testimony. Further reflection led me to: But to get there, we have to be willing to go into the interior, thereby, "recognizing the sacredness of her own female power," *which Lorde places in the feminine plane, and Keating (1992, 31) characterizes as* "physically, emotionally, spiritually . . . divine."

We will get there. But, you know, reprogramming of yourself takes a lot. It takes a lot. It takes the space that I took for myself. Right?!

It just does, and I feel like I had to take that space by hook or by crook, as they say. You have to assert that you need it, but it gave me a time as a mental cleansing process to be like, I can actually crack even in the context of my world.

And so, I get to say, like, look, no, I don't want to rent anymore. So, what does that look like? What challenges my preconceived notions that I cannot have a house. What was it? What was that colonization process that is that you don't deserve it? What was the colonization process that says you're not divine and you don't, you should look [*to*] outward sources as divine more than you? So, you know, I have to investigate. We got to investigate and explore. And sometimes, people are scared to do that work because they're scared of what's going to come out of it.

And Audre Lorde talks about that fear, right? Yeah. And how we impose that fear on ourselves.

Right?

Right! We had help, though. I mean, come on, people. I mean, biblically, even within the spiritual context or even the church, they're like, don't masturbate. What?! I don't get to pleasure myself?! How in the world do you think that I'm supposed to give pleasure to the outside world, and I don't even know what makes this tick?

In Cancer Journals, *Audre Lorde offers her testimony of the role of masturbation in her life (1980, 25). And in this testimony, we see how Lorde not only engages in self-pleasure but also conquers fear—externally generated fear. Through her act of masturbation, Lorde, in essence, challenges what, according to heteronormativity and patriarchy, is illegitimate (see Clarke 1990). In detailing her rediscovery of self-pleasure after surgery, Lorde offers masturbation as an empowering act—an act of claiming one's body and seeing a Black woman's body outside of the narrative that it is to be used for the pleasure of others. Lorde showed us what it means to go into the interior—exploring the knowledge held in feelings and through the act of masturbation.*

I don't get to explore my body. People put so much context on other people giving them pleasure and don't know, like take the time to pleasure ourselves. Which also [*is*] like who gets to own your body? It goes back to body politics and all of the facets where people say you can't, or you don't have a right to abortion.

Because this book of existence says, you're not supposed to get it. No, I actually get rights to my body.

As Lakeesha points out, religion serves as one form of regulating women's sexuality. But what she is getting at is how fear, hegemonic fear, intersects with socially constructed identities and thus exerts, disproportionately, power (see Johnson 2016; Han 2013; Lorde 1984; McClelland and Fine 2008; Zavella 2003). Tamura Lomax (2018), in Jezebel Unhinged, *opined,*

> I learned that the Black Church and black popular culture significantly influence each other, especially in their omnipresent circulating discourse on black womanhood. And I learned that the promulgating of this discourse as "truth" can be just as death dealing, anxiety inducing, and dehumanizing as white supremacist discourses on race. (x)

Lomax pointedly captures how the Black female body is marked and problematized by religion and religious spaces.

Lines.

I remember as a young girl going to vacation Bible school and the teacher telling us that the little girls should sit with our legs closed because the Bible says so. I kept patiently waiting to hear what she would say to the boys. Foolish me for thinking that the Bible would also tell boys how to behave. This was one of my early encounters with lines and how "wildness" was contained.

In the context of heterosexuality, women's sexual pleasure and desires are typically not viewed as relevant or necessary attributes of their sexuality as the purpose of sexuality is constructed as either resting in the realm of reproduction or male sexual pleasure (Vance 1989; Rich 1980). But even this is racialized. Historically, Black women's, and even more so, Black queer women's sexualities, have been subjugated (Petermon and Spencer 2019; Collins 2000, 2005). Stereotypes and scripts written on Black women's bodies result in the construction of the sexually loose Black woman. Consequently, policies are designed to control and monitor their bodies (See Jordan-Zachery 2017; Collins 2000, 2005; Stephens and Phillips 2003; hooks 1992). Thus, Black queer individuals, like Lakeesha, have had to "redefine representation" *(Bailey 2016).*

A rapist has more rights if you're thinking about legal and political; a rapist has more rights to my body, is what you're saying to me than I have rights to my body. So, I feel like, in the context of pleasure, I get to pleasure myself first.

Who owns my body? As a Black woman who owns my body? Capitalism seems to want to take a piece. Legal structures determine what I can do with my body. Organized religion makes its claim to my body. Race-gender constructions also exert pressure in determining who owns my body. Some days, I'm in a constant fight to exert control over my own body. And so, like Blossom, Audre, Lakeesha, and Oya, I constantly have to plough (to borrow from Zora Neale Hurston) my way to self-ownership. This means defining my desires, claiming my pleasure, and situating me politically. And this is the work involved in living the erotic. As I write this, I honor the depth and intensity of the work done by Black women to exist, the work that Lakeesha speaks about. Each day as a Black woman, I myself and in community, nurture and tend my gardens (to borrow from Walker), turning what was meant to be withered into a vibrant green filled with love, hope, resistance, and a deep sense of being fully human. This is the magic that Lakeesha is talking about, that Black women use to make themselves whole.

Feminine: It's within Me

Feminine, what do you think?

So, the first word [*that*] comes to me is genderless.

Because you can be feminine and be a man, be masculine presenting, you can be feminine. I think feminine is the way in which you look at yourself, and you get to define it for you. Because people would look at me sometimes and say [*trails off*]. My good friend Olivia was like, "I thought, I thought you was the stud in the relationship."

I said, "I'm not."

She said, "But you're so aggressive!"

And I was like, me? Being aggressive has nothing to do with me being feminine.

I am feminine. I consider myself as femme. Am I wearing overalls? Sometimes, yes. But am I looking good when I wear my overalls? Yes! All of that is divine! It is divine. It is within me, you know. And I think that we get these notions of what feminine is supposed to be or look like in our society. If a woman does not shave her armpits, she's being less feminine and more masculine, and nothing could be further from the truth. I get to define what is divine and feminine for me.

"I like how you link divine and feminine. Are you aware that you connect those two?"

I do, yes. Yes, I do because it's liberatory! It's all liberation. All self-exploratory. Divine and feminine exist within me.

And since I am divine and I am feminine, it is all me.

There is something so spiritual in the testimony of Lakeesha, especially that last line, "And since I am divine and I am feminine, it is all me." *But being* "me" *is not always as easy as she suggests—the questioning of her identity and the identity of her partnership. Mignon Moore (2006) writes,*

> The ability to appreciate or emulate a particular way of dressing that is masculine does not preclude transgressives or gender-blenders from seeing themselves as women in a society where men still have the greater advantage. They believe that men are constantly granted more status and authority because society continues to advance an ideology that privileges male leadership of important societal institutions and that awards men an earnings advantage that sometimes facilitates their partners' economic dependence. As women, lesbians do not benefit from either of these gendered structural advantages, so relationships organized around gender display do not provide a gendered economic advantage for the less feminine partner. (134)

Moore's writing reflects the boundaries Lakeesha touched on. The boundaries where societally imposed norms of how we should appear and act are constantly in the margins (as understood by hooks). And this can affect our self-articulation and legitimization within our introspective and intimate spheres.

Energy: Messages of the Ancestors

Let's talk about energy.

Cosmos.

So, I feel like we as Black people have what the cosmos has in us, has in the melanin, the stars. The messages the cosmos has to send us. And so, with that is the energy of us as a people. And for so long that has been crushed, that knowledge has been crushed out of us, and I think that people are exploring what that means. I'm always saying my people are going come and get me one day, and for people who are out there like they know they have to believe in like alien forms and beings that like for me, for a long time as a child, I was like, there has to be something that exists beyond this planet. There has to be something that exists beyond the energy of this planet and that they're not telling us. So, I believe that people exist in the cosmos. That energetic pool that you were talking about, that you felt at the lake is an energetic pool of the cosmos[4], is the messages of the ancestors. And I believe that while our physical form goes somewhere at the time of our death, the energy, the cosmic pool is always there. I believe that the energy that we feel when we feel protected and sheltered is the energy of our ancestors letting us know that everything is OK. I believe that when we're fearful and or we're questioning a certain situation, that is the energy of our ancestors to tell us to get out or leave the situation that we don't always believe.

> Each night Blossom learn a new piece of Oya, and finally, it come to she. She had the power to see and the power to fight; she had the power to feel pain and the power to heal. . . . She become a obeah woman, spiritual mother, and priestess of Oya. (Brand 1988, 40, 41)

What happens when the ancestors/spirits speak? And more importantly, what happens if they talk, and we allow ourselves to listen? I come back to Blossom, the central charter in Brand's short story. After she ran, literally, her husband out of the house and took the time to go into the interior, Blossom enters Oya's "lovely womb of strength and fearlessness," *and it was there where she was able to find her truth; her sense of who she was. Remember that Oya is the goddess that leads women to freedom/independence. When Blossom surrendered, Blossom/Oya was able to pursue a successful entrepreneurial career—speakeasy business.*[5] *And she was able, through her use of obeah, to tap into the* "power to fight, power to feel pain and the power to heal."

By going into the interior and allowing the voice of the ancestors/spirits to guide her, Blossom transformed, not just on the micro level but also on the macro level, as the transformation was also about the reckoning of the plight of Black people and how she was able to help them and herself navigate hardship. Blossom had to tap into a particular type of energy. This energy allowed her to transcend the dominant narratives of Western philosophic thought, the energy of the Pentecostal church, to enable Oya to come with her wind. Oya then led her to what she characterizes as a peaceful life—that liberatory self that Lakeesha speaks of. Blossom (like Lakeesha or Lakeesha like Blossom) needed to transcend to resist the lines that limit them by telling them that their knowledge is invalid and that their sense of self is illegitimate. Remember that obeah is frowned upon, especially in the church. Blossom, like Lakeesha, relies on obeah and magic to make themselves real. Using the ancestors and spirits allows Lakeesha to find spiritual liberation and social empowerment. The energy of the cosmos.

Moving outside of lines.

We question ourselves and our thought processes. But I believe that gut instinct is always the energetic pool of the ancestors, saying this is right, this is wrong. And again, we've been colonized out of our intuition on so many different levels.

So, when we talk about a Black woman going into the health care, into the health care system, and is told that she can't trust her body, that she has nothing to fear for the labor process . . . that she should listen to all of the medical professionals and then she ends up dying during childbirth because she did not listen to herself. So, was the energy of the ancestors telling her, you are right, push them to listen to you. But again, the colonization process is thorough. It happens at every level. It happens in the medical-industrial complex. It happens in this military state and police and carceral state that we're in where we have been shamed out of saying Black Lives Matter, and we have been shamed or bullied out of saying, you know, the police are harming us and demanding justice like it is. It is all [*the*] ancestors' energetic presence saying, "stay firm, you are maroon people," you are not crazy, these things that are happening to you. And even if you are crazy, like me, embrace that term, your existence matters!

"Your existence matters." *The emphasis on this assertion,* "your existence matters," *cannot be captured in this book. It was said with conviction, and no question lingered to suggest that Lakeesha may have been seeking permission. Through her, this moment allowed me to see how the ancestors speak and what happens when we listen. The feelings give way to a way of being, an understanding of self. And I would argue that the ancestors can help us access the erotic—they can help us tap into the spiritual, the sensuous, and the political. Thus, they give us the room to name our desires and use our voices for liberation—thus transforming* "silence into language and action" *(Lorde 1984).*

Sacred Moments of Our Existence: The Erotic

Now we come to erotic.

I love the erotic.

"Tell me why you love the erotic. Tell me. Tell me."

Okay, so I love the erotic so much because I get into this massive room with who we are in our very visible moments and our very secret and sacred moments of our existence. And erotic does not have to be sexually erotic, although it is. And that is OK, too. The erotic can be something that fills you up and just gives you this glow like my writing, or when I'm conjuring, it feels very erotic for me. Like, I feel it in my sacral chakra, and it gives me room to breathe and grow and expand. I feel it when I'm making love to my partner, but also when I'm making a good meal for my family, and I'm putting all of the ingredients [*together*], and I'm smelling all of the ingredients. That seems erotic to me. So, there are many uses for the erotic that get us to more freedom and liberation, especially for Black women.

The many spaces of the erotic—writing, conjuring, making a meal, making love . . . the erotic is expansive. The erotic offers Black women, wild Black women, a way to engage the present, allowing the past to meet this present so that they can enter into the future. In essence, the erotic is a psychic, emotional, spiritual, cultural, and sensual link to self and others.

In describing the erotic, Lakeesha centers liberation and social empowerment not just for herself but for Black women. She does the work of bringing Black women to the center (see hooks 1984). In the context of anti-Blackness, patriarchy, capitalism, sexism, and other oppressive structures, the work of subjectivity is not necessarily easy. This work requires that one become a "willful subject" *(Ahmed 2014b). A willful subject engages a practice of questioning and critiquing the lines that society sometimes expects one to exist in. A willful subject can and does engage in disobedience (see Ahmed 2014b). And disobedience is sometimes met with punishment. Lorde speaks to this when she says that the erotic is feared and thus controlled.*

So, what happens when Black women live their erotic? What happens when they tap into their internal power? First, I need to pause and observe that Lakeesha mentions that the erotic means feeling her sacral chakra. The sacral chakra is located in the lower belly, and some place it in the genitalia area. Often associated with feminine energy and the crescent moon, as broadly understood, the sacral chakra governs passion and pleasure. For some, passion and pleasure are relegated to the sexual realm. But there is much more to it than that. As Lakeesha expresses, pleasure and passion can be found in cooking. Thus, it is important to recognize that the sacral chakra speaks to our creativity and sensuality. This particular chakra oversees our sexuality, reproductive processes, relationships—intimate and otherwise—emotions, and our sense of adventure. It is a place of growth and expansion, as Lakeesha describes. By tapping into the erotic and her sacral chakra, Lakeesha accesses a profound set of knowledges that rest outside of Western epistemological patterns; this allows her to vision and create herself as whole. This, combined with the winds of Oya, allows Lakeesha to tend her green pastures, which for her is liberation.

Chapter 7

Talking to the Sugar Canes

What My Gran Taught Me about Seeing Myself

Prelude VII

> There's a place in you that you must keep . . . inviolate. You must keep it, pristine, clean.
>
> —Maya Angelou (in conversation with Oprah Winfrey)

We are in a pandemic. I sit here gazing out of the window, two computers going, my personal laptop and the desktop from work—the one I use when I teach online and attend meetings. And I find myself pondering what am I doing. Higher education's capitalist neoliberal structure seems to want to require or even demand that I "act" as if things are normal. There is a cry to return to "normal," a pre-COVID-19 state. But I look around, and I know and feel that things are other than normal. And I wonder whose normal is the standard? This chapter comes out of this space. It's not a conclusion as such a thing does not exist when we are thinking of testimony. As I stated in the introduction, this book of testimony is like the testimonies my gran often shared. There is no clear ending or beginning—she shares what is necessary in the moment, adding to it over time. And this is how I encourage you to engage with "Talking to the Sugar Canes."

Do not look for a neat conclusion. Do not look for definitive statements declaring "the characteristics of a wild woman include" only to be followed by a list. Instead, this part of the testimony should be engaged with as an entry into the unknown, the known and unknowing, and all the spaces in between where we, Black women, are allowed to see ourselves by venturing into our interior. I am learning that the interior is a portal that allows for exploration and an opportunity to see self—it is that place where feelings rest. And these feelings, when harnessed, can allow us to experience freedom—that freedom to see ourselves, to imagine ourselves in the future as we live in the present.

I have had to wrestle with my feelings as I shelter in place. Not being able to see my grandmother or my mother while recognizing that time, while feeling as if it is standing still, is actually moving. And this is what often led me to sit on my deck reading. Searching the words of Black-identified women for their understanding of freedom. While COVID-19 is new, moving through pandemics is not necessarily new to Black women—I think of HIV/AIDS and the violences Black women endure daily—and I come to the sacred texts that I mentioned in chapter 1 as a way of helping me to make sense of my feelings. I needed to see how Black women, in fiction and other genres, engage the process of self-actualization; how they understand freedom. I had to "see" how they feel. But there is one woman, whose testimony continues to unfold, who was truly my portal into my feelings—my interior, the place I keep inviolate. And this woman is my grandmother.

When My Gran Testifies

I can remember the first time I saw me. And I mean saw me as me and not as Monica and Evan Jordan's child. Not as the little girl who went up the hill to attend Sunday school. Not as the girl/young woman who was a good student. But as me—an individual who was sent to earth whole and with everything she needed. I remember the first time I saw me outside of race-gender structures, or at least as best I could since our lives are dialectical.

The first time I saw me, I was about two and a half or three years old. I asked, or maybe told is a better understanding, my parents to allow me to go to school (I tell this story in chapter 1). I really wanted to go to school, and it was not because I had an older sibling who was attending school. My parents have only one child. But I could see myself in school. As I look back on this, I am unsure where my understanding of school emerged or even how I could see myself. But to be honest, the first time I saw myself was through the eyes of my grandmother.

I was an adult when my gran told me a part of her testimony. I share a bit of it here with you, and yes, with her permission.

My gran's mother died when she was three years old. She had four siblings; my gran was the second youngest and the first of two girls. After her mother died, they were raised by her aunt. Her aunt, by all accounts, was abusive. My gran was the "darker" of the two sisters and, as such, received the brunt of the physical and verbal abuse. That part of the testimony I was privy to for years.

Yet, it would be years before I was made aware of this part of my gran's testimony. My gran ran away from her aunt's house around the age of eleven. An elder took her in. But what that meant was that my gran worked, and worked hard, as a young girl. As we call it in Barbados, she worked in the crop, which means that she would work harvesting sugar canes. She tells me the story of how she headed canes—transporting the canes from the field to the trolley that would then carry them to the plantation. Often, my gran smiled as she recounted these tales. She told me that when she had to head the burnt canes, all one could see were her eyes as she would be covered in soot at the end of the day. From all accounts, my gran was small in stature. In my mind, I picture this pint-sized girl with a head full of hair, a bundle of canes on top of her head trudging through the cane fields. Laden and covered in soot.

But what does this have to do with me seeing myself? As a little girl/young woman, my gran told me how she would walk and talk to the sugar canes. She shared her desires with them. Pouring out her heart to the canes even before she knew there was a god. And the desire she would pour out was that she wanted to see her children grow into adults and see her grandchildren and great-grandchildren. She asked the sugar canes to keep her alive. This is from a little girl whose life was difficult in ways I sometimes cannot comprehend. Yet, she could imagine a future in the here and now. My gran engaged in a type of self-actualization that allowed her not only to see herself in the future while living in the present but that allowed her to see me (and all of us). My grandmother tapped into her interior, that place of her truth, to conjure her lineage.

On March 12, 2021, on Zoom, I had the honor of witnessing my gran's desires—the one she shared with the sugar canes. On that Zoom call were five generations of Harper women.

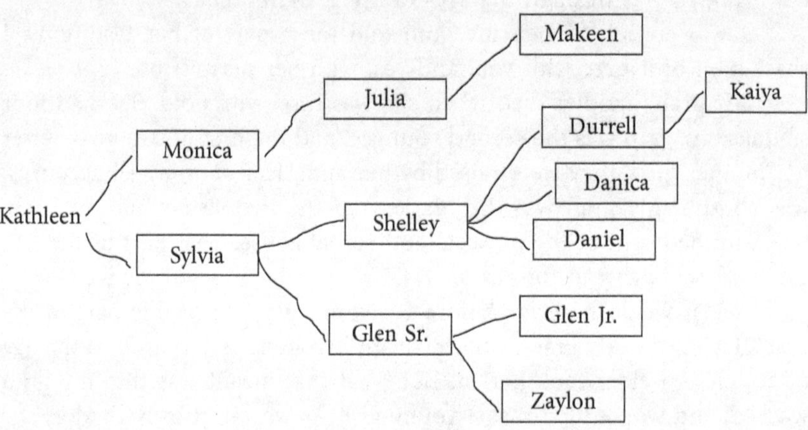

Five generations! Five generations of Harper women connected via fiber optics made real because Kathleen had the audacity to state her desires to the sugar canes (see figure 1). This woman, my gran, named her desires and, more importantly, trusted in her ability to name these desires. At a young age, my grandmother had a belief that was so strong that it seems to defy logic. And on March 12, 2021, I sat in awe, watching her desire—we were present from age nine months to ninety-three years old.

So yes, my gran visioned me. She saw me before I would ever see myself. And as such, she gave me my first understanding of living as a wild Black woman. As my gran would testify, I had no idea she was teaching me about living the erotic—using my feelings to live from my place of truth. Her testimony of speaking her desires to the sugar canes is one example of how Black women tap into the interior to access the erotic. As I have aged and moved through time and space, and as my gran slips away from us—at least in the form that we are most familiar with—I find myself wondering how did that little girl, who faced such tragedies, know how to access her erotic (what I think of as her sacredness)? And I also think what an amazing gift she offered. This is the amazing gift that helped me manage the PTSD I experienced due to the persistent race-gender violences I face. And then I am reminded of how I was able to see me so clearly to declare that I wanted to go to school at the tender age of three. And how the power of naming desires has allowed me to stand here today—through COVID-19, through experiences with Black male patriarchy, through white violence, state-sanctioned violence, anti-Blackness . . . It has allowed me to find my erotic and live as a wild Black woman.

I am hesitant to suggest characteristics and behaviors of what it means to be a wild Black woman. To do such would mean that I am collapsing the erotic and interior into something "measurable." And I want to honor that the interior and the erotic are unique to each woman who chooses to tap into their essence/sacred self. I sat for some time with the question of how do I honor my grandmother and Audre Lorde in this section of *Erotic Testimonies*? Each time I allowed myself to dwell on this question, I would find myself laughing, and I often heard, "Girl, let it be wild!" Girl let it be wild is the opposite of what I have traditionally heard regarding Blackness/womanness. And so, I would close my eyes and imagine what wildness, in the context of Black womanhood, would look like. The image of a burst of colors—yellows, reds, pinks, greens, teals—emerges from deep inside my imagination. Then I was reminded of the following poem I wrote.

Bits and Pieces

i look back
over my shoulder, i see
the bits and pieces of me
the colors and remnants telling
their own tale
testifying.
a Black woman made of several

Black women, cloaked in gold, crimson, and teal
laying there as if discarded
testifying.
the bits and pieces of me, telling
their own tale
a singular tale,
a collective tale,
a generational tale,
spanning centuries and space.
i walk backward in time.
collecting my pieces
the bits and pieces of me
the gold pieces
the crimson pieces
the teal pieces
i lay them out before the ocean
the sunlight cleansing their spirits
the spirits of Black Goddesses emerge
testifying.
each telling their stories
i reach down into my feminine divine
i glimpse a color that I have yet to see
the gold, crimson, and teal have merged to make their own color
a color yet to be defined
just like my Black womanness, the color resists all-encompassing categories
the bits and pieces of me, coming together
testifying.
once fragmented, they find a way to be
whole
mind, body, spirit emerge as the goddess that rules the unknown
as the goddess who resists definitions
emerging as the goddess who shall not be named
ss she is the goddess of Black women
past,
present,
future.

This poem reminds me of the type of archival work that is necessary to tap into the erotic.

Archival Work

Archival Work is.
rich.
deep.
spiritual.
Connected through time and space.
A great awakening.
Restoration.
Sometimes you need a guide,
the ancestors, who rest in the cosmos
to get to know
that your existence matters
as they offer us the energy needed to
define
embodied self, to
push boundaries
throw away boundaries.
As we remember that,
we don't have to walk any line.
Archival work
Unbinds me/us/we, so that we
speak my/our/your truth.
Archival work is
dancing
a joy space
intentional
healing care, and
Being one with the earth,
we become stabilized.
Archival work is
that physical application of magic that
creates something out of nothing.
Crafting
my/our/your own narrative,
sensitive,
to what you feel.
Archival work is
Freedom!

So, what is a wild Black woman? There is no one answer as each woman has to find her truth and stand flat-footed in that truth. The women's testimonies that are shared here capture this. But their words were used to inform the above poem "Archival Work" and help us imagine what being wild feels like and the work involved in being wild—a wild Black woman. Wild is an imaginative mode that empowers Black women with the space to engage in a dialectic practice of negotiating power dynamics that allows them to work to traverse multiple and interlocking forms of oppression. Being wild involves labor and deep stillness.

Individually and collectively, the testimonies, alongside those of Audre Lorde and my gran, offer us a glimpse into how Black women enter their erotic to access their truth. What I noticed is that these women feel and feel deeply. They feel deeply all of their emotions: joy, sadness, ambivalence, longing, and so on. All these feelings rest on the interior, that place that Audre Lorde tells us holds the potential for our freedom.

Audre Lorde's work explores feeling and feeling deeply. I sometimes wonder if we miss this in our interpretation and engagement with her work. Feelings, as she argues, can lead toward self-preservation and what I call self-actualization. Consider Lorde's (1984) words:

> Beyond the superficial, the considered phrase, "It feels right to me," acknowledges the strength of the erotic into a true knowledge, for what that means is the first and most powerful guiding light toward any understanding. And understanding is a handmaiden which can only wait upon or clarify that knowledge, deeply born. The erotic is the nurturer or nursemaid of all our deepest knowledge. (56)

By going into the erotic and nurturing the feelings and the knowledge they hold, Lorde tells us that she is afforded the opportunity to "live from within outward" (1984, 58). By living from "within outward," Lorde informs us that she can address disembodiment. "I am constantly defining my selves, for I am, as we all are, made up of so many different parts. But when those selves war within me, I am immobilized, and when they move in harmony, or allowance, I am enriched, made strong" (Byrd et al. 2009, 156). Harmony and enrichment happen by locating the knowledge that is nestled in her deep feelings.

No blueprint provides us with a method of accessing these deep feelings. And I love that Audre Lorde never told us how to access our erotic. Instead, she invited us to explore our feelings by encouraging us to use our erotic. And that is also something that I have noticed about the women whose testimonies shape this project. Their words act as a portal, entries inviting us to see ourselves—individually and collectively. In essence, their words serve in the same capacity as the words I offered them during our conversations—an opportunity to enter the feeling body. When we enter into the feeling body, we have access to the archives of our truths, and we can use that knowledge to enter into the external world.

Val said, "Don't let the archive dictate what you know." As Lorde and the women suggest, living the erotic involves labor and consciousness. And part of this labor is to engage in archival work. The purpose of archival work is not to keep us in the past but to determine how to use the knowledge. All of these women share the pain and hurts experienced over their lifetimes. But they don't allow the pain to dictate how they live in this moment. That is not to suggest that they ignore or deny the pain; it is acknowledged. However, it is not given center stage. In the same way that whiteness is not given center stage. Lorde writes about pain among other feelings, such as anger, and urged us to allow those feelings to exist but then make a choice of what we want to do with those feelings. This, she argues, is part of the project of self-preservation. In detailing her eighteen-year-old self's experience with abortion, Lorde states that while she was waiting for the fetus to be expelled, there was "a kind of shift from safety towards self-preservation. It was a choice of pains. That's what living was all about. I clung to that and tried to feel only proud. I had not given in" (1982, 111). And we see this shifting in her writings on her experiences with cancer (see *The Cancer Journals*). These shifts, not allowing pain to take center stage, are necessary to engage in "real resistance to the deaths we are expected to live" (Lorde 1984 38). Undergoing these shifts offers Black women a mode of survival and an opportunity to see self—self-actualization—even in the context where their humanity is systematically denied. Self-actualization "is the only substantive mode of survival available to a person pervasively denied value and agency by default structures of her society" (Lorde 1984 38).

Archival work also allows us to step into the power and knowledge of the elders and ancestors. Gloria Wade-Gayles (1993) writes,

> What I remember most vividly from my youth is my respect for women, especially my elders. To me, they were powerful beings, forces that belonged, I thought, to another world, but

> chose to live in this one because we needed them. As blacks, we struggle for personhood and freedom in the physical world, but that was not the only world in which we lived. Women guided us to the other world, the spiritual world, where neither race nor gender was of consequence, and there they nurtured us and made us whole. We called the women wise; they were in fact, spiritual. (248)

The spiritual realm is part of the archives that we have available to us to help us with determining the knowledge held in our feelings. It is part of the toolkit for shifting and seeing self and one way of accessing this spiritual realm is vis-à-vis our ancestors and the elders. We enter into the cosmos as Maya and Lakeesha testify about.

I was always mesmerized when my gran told me how her mother would visit. She would "dream her"—meaning that my gran was not the one doing the dreaming but that her mother would bring her dreams. But then there was a time when my gran turned her back on her mother. I sense that she did not appreciate what her mother was telling her. She would convey with such sadness that she regretted turning her back on her mother as she never again visited. My gran always said she disobeyed. While I listened to her testimony, I found myself wondering what was she being told and what made her "disobey." And I am reminded of the archival knowledge held by the ancestors and how that becomes part of our archive.

I was not surprised when I began to have my own set of dreams. My gran had prepared me; thus, allowing me to access their archive of knowledge—the knowledge that helped me to work through the myriad of feelings I had. My ancestors let me know that I would survive the race-gender violence I faced (see Jordan-Zachery 2019, 2017). We both had archives of pain—the women who visited and me. But we also had knowledge. The ancestors' visits helped me shift. the shifts that Audre Lorde engaged in as she was aborting the fetus and determining how to navigate oppressive structures. These shifts are needed to come deeper into our truths so that the work we do and how we navigate life are not based on others' conceptualizations of whom we ought to be. And they help us to keep our interiors sacred.

Finally, archives are accessed when we are in community—when we can share energy. The archive can be activated in community when energy is mutual, transformative, and generative, as the women discussed through their testimonies. This type of energy is the result of seeing oneself, coming to know self deeply so that one can be in community. The erotic, as Audre Lorde tells us, allows for connections and the types of connections that move outside the boundaries of capitalist, patriarchal, and sexist boundaries. By tapping into the erotic, our deepest feelings, we can move from object to subject, and this is where transcendence resides. In Maya's words, when we enter our interior to access our erotic, we can massage our concerns. Entering the interior provides us with a space for inquiry into our feelings and the opportunity to address our feelings. So, what does this then allow us to do? Sekile says, "I am connected to humanity in a way that it does not feel like work . . . it feels like my purpose." In addition, "I can see past myself, I can see past institutions, past laws, and know that I'm supposed to show up for people," says Sekile. Audre Lorde tells us that our work takes on that quality when we tap into our erotic, and Sekile shows us how.

In thinking of archival work, I borrow from the work of Gay Wilentz, who speaks of constructed knowledge. In the work *Healing Narratives: Women Writers Curing Cultural Dis-ease*, Wilentz, using Brodber's literary method, suggests that constructed knowledge "allow[s] self back into the process of knowing, to confront the pieces of the self that may be experienced as fragmented and contradictory" (2000, 4–5). The erotic is that source of constructed knowledge. It is constructed by our experiences, the experiences of our ancestors and elders, by those we are in community with. Because it resists time as it is past, present, and future, archival work is in the here and now and is metaphysical. It allows us to go into our interior, where our feelings rest. Archival work, often needed to access the interior, allows us to find our truth—the epistemic resources necessary to see ourselves and to navigate life. These feelings that hold our truths can prompt us into action that can lead to our freedom. This gives us an opportunity to act and create a vision of the forward-looking world while being grounded in the present. And this is not Afrofuturism. These women connect with each other, using the feelings resulting from past experiences and understanding of themselves in the future to influence how we live now. Now that is some magic—how they use the archive to create community and, as a result, bend time. Lakeesha would call this conjuring. But, such conjuring requires attentiveness and intentional healing care.

For Lorde, part of living the erotic is spirituality. The erotic is tripartite: spirituality, political, and sensuous. When Black women feel they tap into their spirituality, moving it to the political realm by boldly seeing themselves beyond stereotypes and myths to create themselves. They do this not based on some sense of individualism but instead on their commitment to community and a more just community.

~

Outro

While each woman stands by herself, like the individual colors I see bursting forth, they come together in interesting ways that allow me/us to think of wild through time and space. There are a few elements of their testimonies alongside the testimonies of my gran and Audre Lorde that I find myself reflecting on as I wrap up this portion of this project (I get the sense that *Erotic Testimonies* is not done with me just yet). To allow this section to unfurl and bloom in the way that feels honest and that honors the project, I go back to the testimonies of Maya, Sekile, Val, and Lakeesha and leave you with the following:

"I don't walk anybody's path."—Maya.

"But the thing about the interior is that work is required to get there."—Val

"Feel the vibration."—Sekile

"So, there are many uses for the erotic that gets us to more freedom and liberation, especially for Black women."—Lakeesha.

This is their ode to Black women.

Notes

Feeling, and Deeply

1. I talk a lot about spirituality and being led by the spirit. For me, being led by the spirit means relying on a knowledge/sense that is beyond me and the physical body I am occupying—it is a kind of energy that I tap into. And it is not necessarily religious or grounded in any particular practice, although it could be religious at times. There are multiple definitions of spirituality; one offered by Black feminist Akasha Gloria Hull (2001, 2) suggests that spirituality "involves a conscious relationship with the realm of spirit, with the invisibly permeating, ultimately positive, divine, and evolutionary energies that give rise to and sustain all that exists." I employ this understanding.

Chapter 1

1. I fully recognize that tapping into the interior, one's truth, is not an easy endeavor, and not all can engage in the labor necessary to do such.
2. I rely on poetic inquiry (this is explored more later in this chapter). As a map to reading the poetry, my words are often italicized, direct quotes are indicated with quotation marks, and citations are offered in footnotes so as not to disrupt the poetry.
3. All quotes from Lorde 1984.
4. Complete IRB protocol was followed for all interviews.
5. Lorde 1984.
6. hooks 2000a.
7. Rose 1996, 43.
8. Lorde 1997, "The Winds of Orisha."
9. Lorde 1997, "Between Ourselves."

10. Jordan-Zachery 2019, 79.

11. Soul murder occurs when what is most essential to the person, in my case freedom, human dignity, and the sovereignty to produce knowledge, is killed, but the body is alive. See Schwab 2010.).

12. Lorde 1984, 38.

13. Brown 2013, 14.

14. Lorde 1984, 123.

15. See Griffin 2015; Collins 2000; Guy-Sheftall 1995.

16. Lather 2010.

17. Smith 1985, 10.

18. King 1988.

19. Crenshaw 1991.

20. hooks 1989a.

21. Jordan-Zachery and Harris 2019, 14.

22. Wall 2008, 3.

23. Griffin 2012, 12.

24. Collins 2000.

25. Morgan 2015, 37.

26. Lyric from Grace Jones's song "NightClubbing."

Chapter 2

1. Lyric from Grace Jones's song "NightClubbing."
2. Collins 2000.
3. Jordan-Zachery 2017.
4. Hancock 2004.
5. Jordan-Zachery 2017.
6. Jordan-Zachery 2017, 4.
7. Griffiths 2009.
8. Hull and Smith 1982.
9. McCluney and Rabelo 2019.
10. Ladson-Billings and Donner 2008, 373.
11. hooks 1990.
12. See hooks 1992.
13. hooks 1992, 116.
14. Hammonds 1994, 141.
15. Ryan 2005, 11.
16. Kwakye 2016, 109.
17. LaSalle 2000.
18. Morgan 2015, 36.

Chapter 3

1. This is borrowed from the title of India.Arie's (2013) fifth album *Songversation.*

2. "The Gita is the sixth book of the Mahabharata, one of India's most famous epic poems . . . the Gita recounts a dialogue between Arjuna, one of five Pandava princes, and the Hindu deity Krishna" (Syman 2017).

Chapter 4

1. Sekile, like the other women, was given the opportunity to review her transcript. She offered edits. These edits are included within brackets. Any additions I offer are also included in brackets and are italicized.

Chapter 6

1. I understand the Afrocentric cosmological spiritual system in the way explained by Christel Temple (2012, 23), "The cosmology of Afrocentric womanism regards how Africana women conceptually anticipated freedom and wholeness for African people and how they suspended or deprioritized the value of their present existence in order to predict prophecy and cognitively secure cosmological favor for the race. In other words, acknowledging the ways that Africana women have and continue to ponder, meditate upon, and conceptualize the timelessness of freedom and prosperity for the race is a vital aspect in framing the cosmology of Afrocentric womanism."

2. Lakeesha is a daughter of Yemaya; she tells me this. So, you may wonder if that is Lakeesha's truth, why am I using Oya as part of my embodied reading of her testimony? Oya is not necessarily about Lakeesha and more about me as the recipient of her testimony. This is what the ancestors gave me as a means of engaging Lakeesha's testimony.

3. The use of / does not denote an either/or stance. Instead, it is used to suggest synergy and complementarity.

4. As part of our "introduction," I mentioned to Lakeesha an experience I had as I sat on the shore of a beach in Rhode Island. As I sat at the shore, I was visited by a Black enslaved woman, who, in essence, helped me contextualize the race-gender oppression I was facing during my time in Rhode Island.

5. Blossom's "speak easy" enterprise allows others to stop by to drink, fellowship with others, to witness her when the Oya emerges in her body, and to offer them healing that is beyond religion and capitalist structures.

References

Aghoro, Nathalie. 2018. "Agency in the Afrofuturist Ontologies of Erykah Badu and Janelle Monáe." *Open Cultural Studies* 2: 330–40.

Ahmed, Sara. 2014a. *The Cultural Politics of Emotion*. New York: Routledge Taylor & Francis Group.

———. 2014b. *Willful Subjects*. Durham, NC: Duke University Press.

Alexander, Elizabeth. 2004. *The Black Interior*. Minnesota: Graywolf Press.

Anzaldúa, Gloria, ed. 1990. *Making Face, Making Soul: Creative and Critical Perspectives by Women of Color*. San Francisco: Aunt Lute Foundation Books.

Austin, Regina. 1992. "Black Women, Sisterhood, and the Difference/Deviance Divide." *New England Law Review* 26(3): 877–88.

Badu, Erykah. 2010. "Window Seat." *New AmErykah Part Two: Return of the Ankh*. Universal/Motown.

———. "Window Seat: A Story by Erykah Badu." Dir. Erykah Badu; Co-dir. Coodie & Chike.

Bailey, Moya. 2016. "Redefining Representation." *Screen Bodies* 1(1): 71–86.

Baker-Bell, April. 2017. "For Loretta: A Black Woman Literacy Scholar's Journey to Prioritizing Self-Preservation and Black Feminist–Womanist Storytelling." *Journal of Literacy Research* 49(4): 526–43.

Baker-Fletcher, Karen. 2004. "The Erotic in Contemporary Black Women's Writings." In *Loving the Body: Black Religion/Womanist Thought/Social Justice*, edited by Anthony B. Pinn, and Dwight N. Hopkins, 199–213. New York: Palgrave Macmillan.

Bambara, Toni Cade. 1983. "Toni Cade Bambara." In *Black Women Writers at Work*, edited by Claudia Tate, 12–38. New York: Continuum.

Beauboef-LaFontant, Tamara. 2002. "A Womanist Experience of Caring: Understanding the Pedagogy of Exemplary Black Women Teachers." *Urban Review* 34(1): 71–86.

Beyoncé. 2016. "Formation." Track 12 on *Lemonade*. Parkwood Entertainment and Columbia Records, Studio Album.

Black Girl Bliss. 2018. *Pussy Prayers: Sacred and Sensual Rituals for Wild Women of Color.* Eleven25.

Boyce Davies, Carole. (1994) 1999. *Black Women Writing and Identity: Migrations of the Subject.* New York and London: Routledge.

Brand, Dionne. (1988) 1989. *Sans Souci and Other Stories.* Ithaca NY: Firebrand Books.

Breidenbach, Paul S. 1976. "Colour Symbolism and Ideology in a Ghanaian Healing Movement." *Africa: Journal of the International African Institute* 46(2): 137–45.

Brown, Ruth Nicole. 2013. *Hear Our Truths: The Creative Potential of Black Girlhood.* Urbana: University of Illinois Press.

Byrd, Rudolph P., Johnnetta B. Cole, and Beverly Guy-Sheftall eds. 2009. *I Am Your Sister: Collected and Unpublished Writings of Audre Lorde.* New York: Oxford University Press.

Cardi B featuring Megan Thee Stallion. 2020. "WAP." Single. Atlantic Records.

Carey, Tamika. 2016. *Rhetorical Healing: The Reeducation of Contemporary Black Womanhood.* Albany: State University of New York Press.

Chavers, Linda. 2016. "Here's My Problem with #BlackGirlMagic." *Elle,* January 13, 2016. http://www.elle.com/life-love/a33180/why-i-dont-love-blackgirlmagic/.

Cherry, Kendra. 2020. "Green in Color Psychology." *Very Well Mind.* February 18, 2022. https://www.verywellmind.com/color-psychology-green-2795817.

Clarke, Cheryl. 1990. ". . . She Still Wrote Out the Word Kotex on a Torn Piece of Paper Wrapped Up in a Dollar Bill. . . ." *Conversant Essays: Contemporary Poets on Poetry*, edited by James McCorkle. Detroit: Wayne State University Press, 443–58.

Clarke Hine, Darlene. 1995. "Rape and the Inner Lives of Black Women in the Middle West: Preliminary Thoughts on the Culture of Dissemblance." In *Words of Fire: An Anthology of African American Feminist Thought*, edited by Beverly Guy-Sheftall, 380–88. New York: The New Press.

Collins, Patricia Hill. 2000. *Black Feminist Thought: Knowledge, Consciousness and the Politics of Empowerment*, 2nd ed. New York: Routledge.

———. 2005. *Black Sexual Politics: African Americans, Gender, and the New Racism.* New York: Routledge.

Color Psychology Meaning. n.d. "Color Turquoise." https://colorpsychologymeaning.com/color-turquoise/.

Conquergood, Dwight. 1991. "Rethinking Ethnography: Toward a Critical Cultural Politics." *Communication Monographs* 58: 179–91.

Cooper, Brittney C. 2012. "(Un)Clutching My Mother's Pearls, or Ratchetness and the Residue of Respectability." The Crunk Feminist Collective (blog), December 31, 2012. http://www.crunkfeministcollective.com/2012/12/31/unclutching-my-mothers-pearls-or-ratchetness-and-the-residue-of-respectability/.

———. 2018. *Eloquent Rage: A Black Feminist Discovers Her Superpower.* New York: Picador.

Cooper, Martha, and Nika Kramer. 2005. *We B*Girlz.* New York: Power House Books.

Cooper Owens, Deirdre, and Sharla M. Fett. 2019. "Black Maternal and Infant Health: Historical Legacies of Slavery." *American Journal of Public Health.* 109(10): 1342–45.

Cox, Ida, and Porter Grainger. "One Hour Mama." [1939] 1980. Track 14 on *Mean Mothers: Independent Women's Blues, Volume 1.* Rosetta RR 1300, vinyl LP.

———. "Wild Women Don't Have the Blues." [1924] 1981. Track 1 on *Wild Women Don't Have the Blues. Women's Heritage Series—Foremothers Volume 1.* Rosetta RR 1304, vinyl LP.

Crenshaw, Kimberlé W. 1991. "Mapping the Margins: Intersectionality, Identity Politics, and Violence against Women of Color." *Stanford Law Review* 46(6): 1241–99.

Crenshaw, Kimberlé W., Andre J. Ritchie, Rachel Anspach, Rachel Gilmer, and Luke Harris. 2015. *Say Her Name: Resisting Police Brutality against Black Women.* Digital. New York: African American Policy Forum.

Davis, Angela. 1998. *Blues Legacies and Black Feminism: Gertrude "Ma" Rainey, Bessie Smith and Billie Holiday.* New York: Vintage Books.

Davis, Chie. 2014. "What's Ratchet? And Why Does the Word Need to Die, Like Right Now?" Upworthy. July 11, 2014. https://www.upworthy.com/whats-ratchet-and-why-does-the-word-need-to-die-like-right-now.

Diakantoniou, Maria Theodora. 2018. "'Where Wild Women Grow': Nature, Wildness, and the Search for Identity in Toni Morrison's Jazz." *The Scattered Pelican,* April 29, 2018. https://thescatteredpelican.com/2018/04/29/where-wild-women-grow-nature-wildness-and-the-search-for-identity-in-toni-morrisons-jazz/.

Dill, LeConté J., Shavaun S. Stutton, Bianca Rivera, and Abena Amory-Powell. 2019. "'I Can Only Do Me': African American, Caribbean American, and West African Girls' Transnational Nature of Self-Articulation." In *Black Girl Magic Beyond the Hashtag: Twenty-First-Century Acts of Self-Definition,* edited by Julia S. Jordan-Zachery and Duchess Harris, 60–79. Tucson: University of Arizona Press.

Ellis, Carolyn, and Arthur P. Bochner. 2000. "Autoethnography, Personal Narrative, Reflexivity." In *Handbook of Qualitative Research,* 2nd ed., edited by Norman. K. Denzin and Yvonne. S. Lincoln, 733–68. Thousand Oaks, CA: Sage.

Ewing, Eve L. 2019. *1919.* Chicago: Haymarket Books.

Few, April L., Dionne P. Stephens, and Marlo Rouse-Arnet. 2003. "Sister-to-Sister Talk: Transcending Boundaries and Challenges in Qualitative Research with Black Women." *Family Relations: An Interdisciplinary Journal of Applied Family Studies* 52(3), 205–15.

Fürst, Saskia. 2017. "Palimpsests of Ancestral Memories: Black Women's Collective Identity Development in Short Stories by Edwidge Danticat and Dionne Brand." *English Academy Review,* 34(2), 66–75.

Garner, Porshe. 2019. “Black Girlhood Spirituality: A Definition.” In *Black Girl Magic Beyond the Hashtag: Twenty-First-Century Acts of Self-Definition*, edited by Julia S. Jordan-Zachery and Duchess Harris, 105–25. Tucson: University of Arizona Press.

George, Janel A. 2015. “Stereotype and School Pushout: Race, Gender, and Discipline Disparities in the Context of School Discipline Disparities.” *Arkansas Law Review* 68(1): 101–29.

Gill Lyndon. 2018. Erotic Islands: Art and Activism in the Queer Caribbean. Durham, NC: Duke University Press.

Gleason, Judith. 1987. *Oya: In Praise of the Goddess*. Boston: Shambhala Publication.

Green-Barteet, Miranda A. 2013. “ ‘The Loophole of Retreat’: Interstitial Spaces in Harriet Jacobs’s *Incidents in the Life of a Slave Girl*.” *South Central Review* 30(2): 53–72.

Griffin, Rachel A. 2012. “I AM an Angry Black Woman: Black Feminist Autoethnography, Voice, and Resistance.” *Women’s Studies in Communication* 35(2): 138–57.

———. 2015. “Cultivating Promise and Possibility Black Feminist Thought as an Innovative, Interdisciplinary, and International Framework.” *Departures in Critical Qualitative Research* 4(1): 1–3.

Griffiths, Jennifer L. 2009. *Traumatic Possessions: The Body and Mind in African American Women’s Writings and Performance*. Charlottesville and London: University of Virginia Press.

Guy-Sheftall, Beverly. 1995. *Words of Fire: An Anthology of African-American Feminist Thought*. New York: The New Press.

———. 2002. “The Body Politics: Black Female Sexuality and the Nineteenth-Century Euro-American Imagination.” In *Skin Deep, Spirit Strong: The Black Female Body in American Culture*, edited by K. Wallace-Sanders, 13–63. Ann Arbor: University of Michigan Press.

Hale, Lindsay. 2001. “Mama Oxum: Reflections of Gender and Sexuality in Brazilian Umbanda.” In *Oshun across the Waters: A Yoruba Goddess in Africa and the Americas*, edited by Joseph M. Murphy and Mei Mei Sanford, 241. Bloomington: Indiana University Press.

Hammond, Karla. 1980. “An Interview with Audre Lorde.” *American Poetry Review* 9(2): 18–21.

Hammonds, Evelynn. 1994. “Black (W)Holes and the Geometry of Black Female Sexuality.” *Differences: A Journal of Feminist Cultural Studies* 9(3): 31–45.

Han, C. W. 2013. “Darker Shades of Queer: Race and Sexuality at the Margins.” In *Men Speak Out: Views on Gender, Sex, and Power*, 2nd ed., edited by S. Tarrant, 94–101. New York: Routledge.

Hancock, Ange Marie. 2004. *The Politics of Disgust: The Public Identity of the Welfare Queen*. New York: New York University Press.

Harris, Lakeesha J. 2018. “Healing through (Re)Membering and (Re)Claiming Ancestral Knowledge about Black Witch Magic.” In *Black Women’s Libera-*

tory Pedagogies, edited by O. Perlow, D. Wheeler, S. Bethea, and B. Scott. Palgrave Macmillan, Cham. https://doi.org/10.1007/978-3-319-65789-9_14.

Harris-Perry, Melissa. 2011. *Sister Citizen: Shame, Stereotypes, and Black Women in America*. New Haven, CT: Yale University Press.

Harrison, Rashida. 2019. "Movement Makers: A Historical Analysis of Black Women's Magic in Social Movement Formation." In *Black Girl Magic Beyond the Hashtag: Twenty-First-Century Acts of Self-Definition*, edited by Julia Jordan-Zachery and Duchess Harris, 41–59. Tucson: University of Arizona Press.

Higginbotham, Evelyn Brooks. 1992. "African American Women's History and the Metalanguage of Race." 1992. *Signs* 17(2): 251–274.

Hogan, Linda. 1995. *Dwellings: A Spiritual History of the Living World*. New York: Norton.

Holloway. Karla F. C. 1992. *Moorings and Metaphors: Figures of Culture and Gender in Black Women's Literature*. New Brunswick, NJ: Rutgers University Press.

hooks, bell. 1984. *Black Looks: Race and Representation*. Boston: South End Press.

———. 1989a. *Talking Back: Thinking Feminist, Thinking Black*. Boston: South End Press.

———. 1989b. "Choosing the Margin as a Space of Radical Openness." *Framework: The Journal of Cinema and Media* 36: 15–23.

———. 1990. *Yearning: Race, Gender and Cultural Politics*. Boston: South End Press.

———. 1992. *Black Looks: Race and Representation*. Boston: South End Press.

———. 1993. *Sisters of the Yam: Black Women and Self-Recovery*. Boston: South End Press.

———. 1995. *Killing Rage: Ending Racism*. New York: Holt.

———. 2000a. *Feminist Theory: From Margin to Center*, 2nd ed. London: Pluto Press

———. 2000b. *All about Love*. New York: Harper Perennial.

Hull, Akasha Gloria. 2001. *Soul Talk: The New Spirituality of African American Women*. Rochester, VT: Inner Traditions International.

Hull, Gloria T., and Barbara Smith. 1982. "Introduction: The Politics of Black Women's Studies." In *All the Women Are White, All the Blacks Are Men, But Some of Us Are Brave: Black Women's Studies*, edited by Barbara Smith, Gloria T. Hull, and Patricia B. Scott, xvii–xxi. New York: Feminist Press.

India.Arie. 2013. *Songversation*. Soul Bird Music, Motown Records, cd.

Jackson, Jenn M. 2020. "Private Selves as Public Property: Black Women's Self-Making in the Contemporary Moment." *Public Culture* 32(1): 107–31.

Jaffrey, Zia. 1998. "The Salon Interview—Toni Morrison." February 2, 1998. https://www.salon.com/1998/02/02/cov_si_02int/.

Johnson, E. Patrick. 2016. *No Shade, No Tea: New Writings in Black Queer Studies*. Durham, NC: Duke University Press.

Jones, Grace. 1981. "Nightclubbing." Track 4 on *Nightclubbing*. Island, CD.

Jordan-Zachery, Julia. 2009. *Black Women, Cultural Images and Social Policy*. New York: Routledge.

———. 2017. *Shadow Bodies: Black Women, Ideology, Representation, and Politics.* New Brunswick, NJ: Rutgers University Press.

———. 2019. "Licking Salt: A Black Woman's Tale of Betrayal, Adversity, and Survival." *Feminist Formations* 31(1): 67–84.

Jordan-Zachery, Julia, and Nikol Alexander-Floyd, eds. 2018. *Black Women in Politics: Demanding Citizenship, Challenging Power, and Seeking Justice.* Albany, NY: State University of New York Press.

Jordan-Zachery, Julia, and Duchess Harris, eds. 2019. "Introduction. We Are Magic AND We Are Real: Exploring the Politics of Black Femmes, Girls and Women's Self-Articulation." In *Black Girl Magic Beyond the Hashtag: Twenty-First-Century Acts of Self-Definition*, 3–40. Tucson: University of Arizona Press.

Keating, Analouise. 1992. "Making 'Our Shattered Faces Whole': The Black Goddess and Audre Lorde's Revision of Patriarchal Myth." *Frontiers: A Journal of Women Studies* 13(1): 20–33.

———. 2000. "The Intimate Distance of Desire: June Jordan's Bisexual Inflections." *Journal of Lesbian Studies* 4(2): 81–93.

King, Deborah. K. 1988. "Multiple Jeopardy, Multiple Consciousness: The Context of a Black Feminist Ideology." *Signs* 14(1): 42–72.

Kraft, Marin. (1986) 2004. "The Creative Use of Difference." In *Conversations with Audre Lorde*, edited by Joan Wylie Hall, 146–54. Oxford: University of Mississippi Press.

Kripalu Center for Yoga and Health. n.d. "Maya Breuer. https://kripalu.org/presenters-programs/presenters/maya-breuer Accessed December 29, 2020.

Kwakye, Chamara. 2016. "From Vivi with Love: Studying the Great Migration." In *The Fluid Boundaries of Suffrage and Jim Crow: Staking Claims in the American Heartland*, edited by Damaris Hill, 105–20. Lanham, MD: Lexington Books.

Ladson-Billings, Gloria, and Jamel K. Donnor. 2008. "Waiting for the Call: The Moral Activist Role of Critical Race Theory Scholarship." In *Handbook of Critical and Indigenous Methodologies, edited by* Norman Denzin, Yvonna Lincoln, and Linda Tuhiwai Smith, 61–83. Thousand Oaks, CA: Sage.

LaSalle, Denise. 2000. "Lick It before You Stick It." Track 2 on *This Real Woman*. Ordena Records, CD.

Lather, Patti. 2010. "Foucauldian Scientificity: Rethinking the Nexus of Qualitative Research and Educational Policy Analysis." *Journal of International Journal of Qualitative Studies in Education* 19(6): 783–91.

Lawuyi, O. B. 1998. "Water, Healing, Gender and Space in African Cosmology." *South African Journal of Ethnology*, 21(4): 185–90.

Lebovits, Susan Chaityn. 2010. "YJ Interview: Maya Breuer on Yoga for Everyone." *Yoga Journal*. February 28, 2010. https://www.yogajournal.com/philosophy/yj-interview-yogi-to-the-people/.

Leggo, Carl. 2008. "Astonishing Silence." In *Handbook of the Arts in Qualitative Research: Perspectives, Methodologies, Examples, and Issues*, edited by J. Gary Knowles and Ardra L. Cole, 165–74. New York: Sage.

Lespinasse, Patricia G. 2010. *The Jazz Text: Wild Women, Improvisation, and Power in 20th Century Jazz Literature.* PhD diss. New York, Columbia University.

Letcher, Lazarus Nance. 2018. "Transgender Murder Memorials: A Call for Intersectionality and Trans Livability." https://digitalrepository.unm.edu/amst_etds/62

Lomax, Tamura. 2018. Jezebel Unhinged: Loosing the Black Female Body in Religion and Culture. Durham, NC; Duke University Press.

Lorde, Audre. 1978. "A Litany for Survival." The Poetry Foundation. https://www.poetryfoundation.org/poems/147275/a-litany-for-survival.

———. 1980. *The Cancer Journals.* San Francisco: Aunt Lute Books.

———. 1982. *Zami: A New Spelling of My Name.* Freedom, CA: The Crossing Press.

———. 1984. *Sister Outsider: Essays and Speeches.* Trumansburg, NY: Crossing Press.

———. 1995. *Black Unicorn: Poems by Audre Lorde.* New York: W. W. Norton & Company Inc.

———. 1997. *The Collected Poems of Audre Lorde.* New York: W. W. Norton.

———. 2017. *Your Silence Will Not Protect You.* London: Silver Press.

McClelland, S. I., and M. Fine. 2008. "Rescuing a Theory of Adolescent Sexual Excess: Young Women and Wanting." In *Next Wave Cultures: Feminism, Subcultures, Activism,* edited by A. Harris, 83–102. New York: Routledge.

McCluney, Courtney, and Verónica Rabelo. 2019. "Conditions of Visibility: An Intersectional Examination of Black Women's Belonginess and Distinctiveness at Work." *Journal of Vocational Behavior* 11(3): 143–52.

McEachern, Montinique D. 2017. "Respect My Ratchet: The Liberatory Consciousness of Ratchetness." *Departures in Critical Qualitative Research* 6(3): 78–89.

McLauchlan, Laura. 2018. "Lively Collaborations: Feminist Reading Group Erotics for Livable Futures Transformations." *Journal of Inclusive Scholarship and Pedagogy*, 28(1): 86–95.

Meggs, Michelle. 2001. "Is There Room for the Ratchet in the Beloved Community? If You're Not Liberating Everyone, Are You Really Talking About Freedom?" In *Womanist Ethical Rhetoric: A Call for Liberation and Social Justice in Turbulent Times*, edited by A. Madlock and C. Glenn, 63–76. Lanham, MD: Lexington Books.

Mittlefehldt, Pamela J. 2003. "Writing the Waves, Sounding the Depths: Water as Metaphor and Muse." *Interdisciplinary Studies in Literature and Environment* 10(1): 137–42. Oxford University Press.

Molina, Maria. L. 1994. "Fragmentations: Meditations on Separatism." *Signs* 19(2): 449–57.

Moore, Mignon R. 2006. "Lipstick or Timberlands? Meanings of Gender Presentation in Black Lesbian Communities." *Signs: Journal of Women in Culture and Society* 32(1): 113–39.

Moreno, Samantha. 2017. "The Enduring Significance of Harriet Powers' Quilts." Artstor, July 7, 2017. https://www.artstor.org/2017/07/07/the-enduring-significance-of-harriet-powers-quilts/.

Morgan, Joan. 2015. "Why We Get Off: Moving Towards a Black Feminist Politics of Pleasure." *The Black Scholar* 45(4): 36–46.

Morris, Monique. 2016. *Push Out: The Criminalization of Black Girls in Schools*. New York & London: the New Press.

Morrison, Toni. 1992. *Jazz*. New York: Alfred A. Knopf.

———. (1987) 2004. *Beloved*. New York: Vintage Books.

Mullings, Leith. 2000. "African-American Women Making Themselves: Notes on the Role of Black Feminist Research." *Souls: A Critical Journal of Black Politics, Culture, and Society* 2(4): 18–29.

Mullins, Katie. 2012. "'My Body is History': Embodying the Past, Present, and Future in Dionne Brand's Sans Souci and Other Stories." *A Review of International English Literature* 42(2): 5–22.

National Organization of Women (n.d.). "Black Women and Sexual Violence." https://now.org/wp-content/uploads/2018/02/Black-Women-and-Sexual-Violence-6.pdf

Nzinga-Johnson, Sekile, ed. 2013. *Laboring Positions: Black Women, Mothering, and the Academy*. Demeter Press.

Otero, Solimar, and Toyin Falola, eds. 2014. "Introduction: Introducing Yemoja." In *Yemoja: Gender, Sexuality, and Creativity in the Latina/o and Afro-Atlantic Diasporas*, xvii–xxii. Albany: State University of New York Press.

Personal Introduction to Santeria. (n.d.) http://www.swarthmore.edu/Humanities/ychirea1/yemaya.html Accessed December 17, 2020

Petermon, Jade, and Leland G. Spencer. 2019. "Black Queer Womanhood Matters: Searching for the Queer Herstory of Black Lives Matter in Television Dramas." *Critical Studies in Media Communication* 36(4): 339–56.

Pickens, Therí A. 2015. "Shoving Aside the Politics of Respectability: Black Women, Reality TV, and the Ratchet Performance." *Women and Performance: A Journal of Feminist Theory*, 25(1), 41–58.

Prendergast, Monica. 2006. "Found Poetry as Literature Review: Research Poems on Audience and Performance." *Qualitative Inquiry* 12(2): 369–88.

Prendergast, Monica, Carl Leggo, and Pauline Sameshima, eds. 2009. *Poetic Inquiry: Vibrant Voices in the Social Sciences*. Boston: Sense Publishers.

Quashie, Kevin E. 2012. *Sovereignty of Quiet: Beyond Resistance in Black Culture*. New Brunswick, NJ: Rutgers University Press.

Rainey, Ma. "Prove It on Me Blues." Recorded 1928. Paramount Records, 12668, vinyl LP.

Ramgopal, Lakshmi. 2016. "'Go and Reclaim Your Tools': Meet the Woman Behind Black Witch University." https://www.vice.com/en/article/a3wddk/go-and-reclaim-your-tools-meet-the-woman-behind-black-witch-university.

Rich, Adrienne. 1980. "Compulsory Heterosexuality and Lesbian Existence." *Signs* 5(4): 631–60

Richards, Sandra L. 2009. "Space, Water, Memory: Slavery and Beaufort, South Carolina." *Cultural Dynamics* 21(3): 255–82. https://doi.org/10.1177/0921374008350381.

Richardson, Elaine. 2002. "To Protect and Serve: African American Female Literacies." *College Composition and Communication* 53(4): 675–704.

———. 2003. *African American Literacies*. New York: Routledge.

Roberts, Dorothy. 1997. *Killing the Black Body: Race, Reproduction, and the Meaning of Liberty.* New York: Vintage Books.

Robinson, Jessica. 2019. "Conjuring Ghosts: Black Girlhood Haunting and Speculative Performances of Reappearance." In *Black Girl Magic Beyond the Hashtag: Twenty-First-Century Acts of Self-Definition*, edited by Julia S. Jordan-Zachery and Duchess Harris, 126–46. Tucson: University of Arizona Press.

Rose, Shirley K. 1996. "What's Love Got to Do with It? Scholarly Citation as Courtship Ritual." *Language and Learning Across the Disciplines* 1(3): 34–48.

Ryan, Judylyn S. 2005. *Spirituality as Ideology in Black Women's Film and Literature.* Charlottesville: University of Virginia Press.

Salt-N-Pepa. 1986. "Push It." On *Hot, Cool & Vicious.* Written by Hurby Azor and Ray Davies. Next Plateau Records. London Recordings. Vinyl.

———. 1993. "Shoop." On *Very Necessary.* Next Plateau Records. London Recordings. Vinyl.

Schram, Sandford F., Joe Soss, Richard C. Fording, and Linda Houser. 2009. "Deciding to Discipline: Race, Choice, and Punishment at the Frontlines of Welfare Reform." *American Sociological Review* 74(3): 398–422.

Schwab, Gabriele. 2010. *Haunting Legacies: Violent Histories and Transgenerational Trauma.* New York: Columbia University Press.

The Sentencing Project. 2020. "Incarcerated Women and Girls." November 24, 2020. https://www.sentencingproject.org/publications/incarcerated-women-and-girls/.

Shange, Ntozake. 1982. *Sassafrass, Cypress & Indigo*. New York: St. Martin's.

———. 1997. *For Colored Girls Who Considered Have Considered Suicide/When the Rainbow Is Enuf.* New York: Simon & Schuster.

Smith, Barbara. 1985. "Some Home Truths on the Contemporary Black Feminist Movement." *The Black Scholar* 16(2): 4–13.

Sosulski, Marya R., Nicole T. Buchanan, and Chandra M. Donnell. 2010. "Life History and Narrative Analysis: Feminist Methodologies Contextualizing Black Women's Experiences with Severe Mental Illness." *Journal of Sociology and Social Welfare* 37(3): 29–57.

Spry, Tami. 2011. *Body, Paper, Stage: Writing and Performing Autoethnography.* Walnut Creek, CA: Left Coast Press.

Stewart, Terah J., and Roshaunda L. Breeden. 2021. " 'Feeling Good as Hell': Black Women and the Nuances of Fat Resistance." *Fat Studies* 10(3): 221–36. https://www.tandfonline.com/doi/full/10.1080/21604851.2021.1907964.

Stephens, D. P., and L. D. Phillips. 2003. "Freaks, Gold Diggers, Divas, and Dykes: The Sociohistorical Development of Adolescent African American Women's Sexual Scripts." *Sexuality and Culture* 7: 3–49.

Summer, Donna. "Love to Love You Baby." Recorded August 1975. Track 1 on *Love to Love You Baby*. Oasis Records.

Syman, Stefanie. 2007. "Bhagavad Gita: The Timeless First Book of Yoga." *Yoga Journal*. https://www.yogajournal.com/yoga-101/first-book-yoga/.

Taylor, Janette. 1998. "Womanism: A Methodological Framework for African American Woman." *Advances in Nursing Sciences* 21(1): 53–64. http://ovidsp.tx.ovid.com.lp.hscl.ufl.edu/sp-3.13.0b/ovidweb.cgi.

———. 2005. "No Resting Place: African American Women at the Crossroads of Violence." *Violence Against Women* 11: 1473–89.

Temple, Christel N. 2021. "The Cosmology of Afrocentric Womanism." *Western Journal of Black Studies* 36(1): 23–32.

Thompson, Robert Farris. 2001. "Orchestrating Water and the Wind: Oshun's Art in Atlantic Context." In *Oshun Across the Waters: A Yoruba Goddess in Africa and the Americas* edited by Joseph M. Murphy and Mei Mei Sanford. Bloomington: Indiana University Press, 261.

Vance, Carole S., ed. 1989. *Pleasure and Danger: Exploring Female Sexuality.* Pandora Press

Vrettos, Athena. 1989. "Curative Domains: Women, Healing and History in Black Women's Narratives." *Women's Studies: An Interdisciplinary Journal* 16(3/4): 455–473.

Wade-Gayles, Gloria. 1993. *Pushed Back to Strength: A Black Woman's Journey Home*. Boston: Beacon Press.

Walker, Alice. 1976. *Meridian*. New York: Pocket Books.

———. 1982. *The Color Purple*. New York: Harcourt Brace Jovanovich.

———. 1983. *In Search of Our Mothers' Gardens: Womanist Prose.* San Diego: Harcourt.

———. 1989 (August). Interview by Claudia Dreifus. "Alice Walker: Writing to Save My Life." *The Progressive* 53: 29–32.

Wall, Sarah. 2008. "An Autoethnography on Learning about Autoethnography." *International Journal of Qualitative Methods* 15(2): 146–60.

Wallace-Sanders, Kimberly. 2002. *Skin Deep, Spirit Strong: The Black Female Body in American Culture.* Ann Arbor: University of Michigan Press.

Washington, Mary Helen. 1990. " 'The Darkened Eye Restored:' Notes Toward a Literary History of Black Women." *Reading Black, Reading Feminist,* edited by Henry Louis Gates, Jr., 30–43. New York: Meridian Books.

Weir-Soley, Donna Aza. 2009. *Eroticism, Spirituality, and Resistance in Black Women's Writings*. Gainesville: University Press of Florida.

Wilentz, Gay. 2000. *Healing Narratives: Women Writers Curing Cultural Dis-ease*. Piscataway, NJ: Rutgers University Press, 2000.

Williams, Terry Tempest. 1995. *Desert Quartet: An Erotic Landscape*. New York: Pantheon.

Young, Thelathia "Nikki." 2012. ""Uses of the Erotic' for Teaching Queer Studies." *Women's Studies Quarterly* 40(3/4): 301–5.

Zavella, P. 2003. "Talkin' Sex: Chicanas and Mexicanas Theorize about Silences and Sexual Pleasure." In *Chicana Feminisms: A Critical Reader*, edited by G. F. Arredondo, A. Hurtado, N. Klahn, O. Najera-Ramirez, and P. Zavella, 228–59. Durham, NC: Duke University Press.

Index

www.ingramcontent.com/pod-product-compliance
Lightning Source LLC
LaVergne TN
LVHW050153080826
844660LV00002B/197

* 9 7 8 1 4 3 8 4 9 1 1 7 2 *